# The Boston Globe

# Cheap Eats

## 52 REAL MEAL DEALS IN GREATER BOSTON

Published by *The Boston Globe*

# The Boston Globe

Copyright © 2008 by The Boston Globe. All rights reserved. No part of this publication may be reproduced, stored in a retrieval system, or transmitted in any form by any means, electronic, mechanical, photocopying, or otherwise, without prior written permission of the publisher, The Boston Globe, PO Box 55819 Boston, MA 02205-5819.

This book is available in quantity at special discounts for your group or organization. For further information, contact:

**The Boston Globe Store**
PO Box 55819
Boston, MA 02205-5819
Phone: (888) 665-2667
Fax: (617) 929-7636
www.BostonGlobeStore.com

Printed in U.S.A.
ISBN 13: 978-0-9790137-8-2

*The factual information listed in this guidebook was confirmed at press time, but is subject to change. We therefore recommend that you call ahead or visit each restaurant online for the most up-to-date prices, menus, and other information. Reviews reflect the experiences and opinions of the writers, which may or may not match reader experiences and opinions.*

**EDITOR** Janice Page
**DESIGNER** Rena Anderson Sokolow
**ASSISTANT EDITOR** Andrea Pyenson

**SPECIAL THANKS** The Boston Globe Living/Arts Department; Nancy Callahan, MacDonald & Evans.

**COVER PHOTO** Anna Buonopane, chef-owner of Pescatore Seafood in Somerville, shows off her golden fried calamari.
Photo by Tom Herde, The Boston Globe.

# Everyone likes a bargain

when they go out to eat — a satisfying meal that doesn't break the bank, an evening where everything is so casual, you don't have to worry about what to wear or who will be there. ❖ Lucky for us, Greater Boston is a mecca for cheap dining, partly because of the student population and partly because of our inherent frugality. What defines Cheap Eats is that almost everything on the menu is $15 or less. So whether you're on a strict budget or simply someone who likes to discover new cuisines, there's something here for you. ❖ Many spots in this edition of "Cheap Eats: 52 Real Meal Deals in Greater Boston" are ethnic mom-and-pops, where he's cooking and she's seating you (or vice versa). Some of these places were opened to cater to their own communities; now we get to reap the benefits. Restaurants such as Annapurna, where the specialties are Himalayan; Tashi Delek, where the menu is Tibetan; and Saray Restaurant, home to Turkish dishes, teach us about cuisines we may not have known before, and about culture, too. ❖ Other places are located where we expect inexpensive dining, such as Gitlo's Dim Sum Bakery in Allston, the reverse of the Chinatown dim sum scene; or Hall of Famer El Pelon Taqueria, in the Fenway, where the Red Sox reign. ❖ Our Cheap Eats reviewers are always on the lookout for places that give you value for your money. Often the tables are small and jammed in, and sometimes you can see remnants of the pizza joint the new place took over. But you're amazed by how good the food is. Whether you're working your way through college or sitting on top of the world, no one can pass up terrific Peruvian pollos a la brasa, rotisserie chicken roasted over hot coals; gyros, with spicy, grilled meat wrapped in thick, homemade pita with garlic-yogurt sauce, tzatziki, lettuce, and tomatoes; or a perfect burger cooked just right, with or without cheese, bacon, and onions on top. Put your appetite to work on a year's worth of Cheap Eats.

SHERYL JULIAN, *Food Editor*, *THE BOSTON GLOBE*

# Annapurna

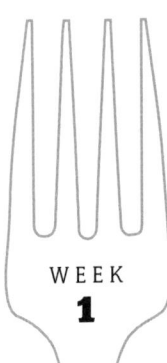

**WEEK 1**

*2088 Massachusetts Avenue, Cambridge*
*617-876-8664*
*www.annapurna2088.com*
*All major credit cards accepted. Entrance wheelchair accessible; bathroom not accessible.*

**PRICES** *Appetizers: $4-$7.49. Entrees: $9-$15. Desserts: $4-$5.*

**HOURS** *Sun-Thu 11 a.m.-10 p.m., Fri-Sat 11 a.m.-11 p.m.*

### HEY, TRY THESE

Vegetarian soup, potato bowlani, chicken or vegetarian momo, chicken sekuwa, chicken kebab, vegetable pakora, Terai curry, Himalayan lamb masala, saag cheese, mantwo, kaddo, bamia, kulfi.

TASTING NOTES

BOSTON • CAMBRIDGE

**BRIHASPATI LAMA, OWNER AND CHEF** of the Cambridge restaurant Annapurna, holds out a plastic Solo cup to a visitor. It is filled with his most prized spice, Nepal's pungent native variety of Szechuan pepper, known as timur. "People here, they don't know this," says Lama, pointing to the jet-black peppercorns. "But in the mountains, we know it." ❖ And now, after a few visits to this pan-Himalayan restaurant, we also know it, and crave it. Timur is intensely aromatic — and, for spice lovers, addictive. ❖ Lama, who hails from Nepal, has made it possible to taste the high-mountain cuisines of Nepal, India, and Tibet without hiring a sherpa. His menu ranges from Himalayan dumplings and warming Tibetan soups to spicy Nepali kebabs and fragrant Indian curries. He also kept part of the Afghan menu served by Ali Baba Tandoor, the restaurant that occupied the space before him. ❖ What unifies them all is Lama's devotion to the light, healthy, aromatic cooking he grew up with at the foot of Annapurna Mountain in Kavrepalanchok, Nepal. Homemade yogurt replaces butter and cream, water often fills in for oil, and steam is preferred to the deep fryer. Flavor comes from fresh ingredients and house-ground spices, not fat, and the result seems part ethnic restaurant, part health spa. ❖ An entree of saag cheese ($8.99), for example, is far lighter than its flatland cousin, the cream-laden Indian saag paneer. Steamed momo dumplings ($5) come Nepali style, with delicate pot-sticker-like wrappers pinched into half-moons and stuffed with juicy, cilantro-flecked fillings of herb chicken or cabbage, offered with a tangy achar, tomato chutney, for dipping. Lama stops by our table to tell us the achar will change often. Sometimes he will make tomato achar, or parsnip or mango. ❖ Other menu hits make up for the drab yellow decor. Himalayan lamb masala ($10.99) delivers tender meat in a nicely caramelized stew of tomatoes and onion. From Nepal's flatlands, Terai chicken ($8.99) is a light, coconut and tomato curry perky with nutmeg. Crisp bamia okra ($5) tickles the tongue with its spices, and fat, juicy chicken kebabs ($11), made with cinnamon, cardamom, and cumin, are a delight. ❖ Salads, however, are so spartan they'd fit in at Everest base camp. Try the potato bowlani, a stuffed pastry ($5); sweet kaddo ($5), the popular Afghan pumpkin dish; butternut squash; and the savory mantwo ($11), which are beef ravioli — but not all on one visit. ❖ Meanwhile, the flavor adventure won't stop with timur. And you don't have to don crampons and hike up a mountain to try them.

DENISE TAYLOR, *Globe Correspondent*

SOMERVILLE • BEYOND

# Orinoco

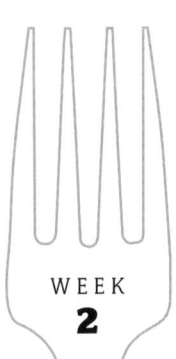

WEEK **2**

*22 Harvard St., Brookline*
*617-232-9505*
*www.orinocokitchen.com*
*All major credit cards accepted.*
*Wheelchair accessible.*
**PRICES** *$4.25-$19 (most dishes under $15).*
**HOURS** *Tue-Sat 11:30 a.m.-2:30 p.m. and 5:30-10 p.m., Sun 11 a.m.-3 p.m. and 5:30-9:30 p.m.*
**ALCOHOL** *Full liquor license.*

### HEY, TRY THESE

Tostones, arepa domino, empanada verde, palmito salad, adobo chicken, polvorosa de pollo, flan.

**TASTING NOTES**

BOSTON • CAMBRIDGE

**THERE ARE SOME RESTAURANTS** I like enough that I idly wish they were closer to my neighborhood. Orinoco is that rare find: an affordable restaurant with spectacular food in a stylish space with a vibrant scene. The restaurant, sibling of the popular South End space opened two years ago by Andres Branger and chef Carlos Rodriguez, is not without its faults. On a couple of visits, the space is buzzing and the energy is infectious. But people are lined up waiting for tables, and the din is overwhelming at the U-shaped bar facing the windows. ❖ The service during the dinner rush is friendly but haphazard. Any annoyance disappears, though, the minute you take a bite of the food. It's inspired by Venezuelan roadside specialties, and it's also just plain inspired. ❖ We start with tostones ($4.25). Green plantain rounds are twice-fried and flattened into golden discs, served with creamy garlic mojo. You really can't eat just one. ❖ Arepas, grilled, stuffed corn flour rounds are a staple in Venezuela. The domino ($5.75) is filled with smoky black beans (some of the meatiest, most satisfying I've tasted) and mild palmizulia cheese. ❖ Another typical Latin American dish is empanadas, a sort of turnover. The pastry for the verde empanada ($7.95) is made with plantains, and it's filled with juicy mushrooms, manchego cheese, and salsa verde. ❖ Panela, raw sugar, shows up in several specialties, including the asado negro ($12.95), chunks of beef slow-cooked with panela and onions, and polvorosa de pollo ($13), a stew of shredded chicken in sweet-savory, cinnamon-y sauce stuffed into a round pastry. ❖ Flan and molten chocolate cake are the only desserts. We're always looking for the perfect flan, so we try quesillo ($4.25) on each visit. This Venezuelan version has nice eggy, vanilla, and burnt caramel flavors, but twice the custard is tough and grainy. The third time's the charm — perfect, firm but silky custard. ❖ Drinks can be hit or miss. On one visit, we get a chokingly strong caipirinha and a perfect mojito, on another we get a perfect caipirinha and a too-sugary, too weak mojito (same bartender) — but you can always order Negra Modelo, a fine dark Mexican lager, or the sangria, so popular it's gone before we get around to ordering a glass. The many regulars at the bar greeting each other and chatting with the bartender obviously share my enthusiasm for this gem. Now where are those Brookline real estate listings?

ANN LUISA CORTISSOZ, *Globe Staff*

SOMERVILLE • BEYOND

# Falafel King

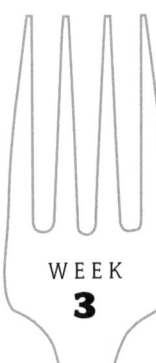

**WEEK 3**

*1504 Hancock St., Quincy*
*617-773-0100*
*MasterCard, Visa accepted. Entrance wheelchair accessible; restrooms are not.*
**PRICES** *Sandwiches: $3.99-$5.75. Salads: $5-$6.50. Entrees: $6.50.*
**HOURS** *Mon-Fri 11 a.m.-9 p.m., Sat 11 a.m.-8 p.m.*
**ALCOHOL** *None.*

### HEY, TRY THESE

Baba ghanouj, falafel-tabbouleh combo sandwich, combo plate, kafta or lamb shish kebabs, chicken shawarma, hummus salad, stuffed grape leaves.

TASTING NOTES
_____
_____
_____
_____

BOSTON • CAMBRIDGE

"**TRY MY FALAFEL!**" ❖ Grinning and holding out a golden-brown ball of deep-fried falafel in each gloved hand, Hassan Alzubaidy is ready for us the moment we walk into the new Quincy Falafel King. ❖ Alzubaidy's fried, meatball-size, house-made falafel is tinged green with aromatic helpings of fresh parsley and cilantro mashed into the nutty-tasting legumes. His cooking is careful and from scratch — just like his brother Kadhim's. In 1999, Kadhim opened the first Falafel King in Downtown Crossing and ever since, the lunch crowd has lined up for his tasty, lightning-fast Middle Eastern takeout. Hassan Alzubaidy meanwhile opened Middle Eastern Grocery & Halal Meat in Quincy, where he also served falafel to in-the-know fans. But the two come from a restaurant family. Back home in Iraq, their father and six brothers also have (or had) restaurants. So Alzubaidy opened one too. "It's my dream," he says. ❖ The menu is the same as the downtown location, with lower prices. We work our way through the kebabs, salads, sandwiches, and the usual Middle Eastern sides like hummus and tabbouleh. Ingredients are impeccably fresh, spices have oomph because they are ground in house. ❖ Each type of kebab or shawarma ($5.75 for a sandwich, $6.50 for a plate) has its own marinade. Moist chicken shawarma, hot off the grill, is perky with lemon, cilantro, and allspice. Tender kafta kebabs — an Iraqi favorite made of flattened, grilled beef and lamb meatballs — are mouth-wateringly savory with cumin, onion, parsley, and scallion. Garlic and allspice bring out the flavor of the lamb kebabs, which are cooked to order. ❖ Vegetarians will find smoky baba ghanouj, light and fluffy with good olive oil, sesame tahini, and just the right amount of lemon to brighten it. Creamy-smooth chickpea hummus melts on the tongue with clean lemon and garlic flavors. ❖ Baba ghanouj, hummus, and tabbouleh all come on the generous combo plate ($6.50), along with broth-cooked rice pilaf, stuffed grape leaves, and, the jewel in the crown, falafel. Combo sandwiches ($5 to $5.99) let you mix and match fillings. ❖ Just about everything comes as a salad, a dinner plate, or a sandwich swaddled in soft, thin pita bread. It's food good enough to bond with strangers over. Toward the end of our meal, a different voice addresses us as we sit at one of the five simple tables munching happily. ❖ "It's good isn't it?" asks a smiling couple about to depart. "I've been a fan of his for years," says the man. "You could say I'm a groupie." You can say that about us too.

DENISE TAYLOR, *Globe Correspondent*

# Four Burgers

WEEK **4**

704 Massachusetts Ave., Central Square, Cambridge

617-441-5444

www.fourburgers.com

MasterCard and Visa accepted. Restrooms not accessible.

**PRICES** *Burgers: $7-$8.50. Sides: $1.50-$3.50. Desserts: $1.50-$6.*

**HOURS** *Mon-Wed 11 a.m.-10 p.m., Thu-Sat 11 a.m.-11 p.m., Sun noon-10.*

**ALCOHOL** *Wine and beer.*

## HEY, TRY THESE

Beef burger, turkey burger, salmon burger, house fries, sweet potato fries, chocolate chip cookies, chocolate milkshake.

TASTING NOTES

BOSTON • CAMBRIDGE

**THERE ARE PROBABLY RESTAURANTS** like Four Burgers opening up all over the country. Who doesn't want a great burger? All it takes is an entrepreneur savvy enough to source food at the best places and, of course, the right real estate.

❖ In this case, the place is in Central Square, in a spot that once housed the Ghandi Restaurant. Four Burgers is bright, clean, and spare. And it's located between two Whole Foods Markets, owner Michael Bissanti points out. ❖ Bissanti makes his four burgers with ingredients you might find at these natural foods markets. The idea here is that the menu is very limited — four burgers, four sides, and a couple of ice cream desserts and cookies. ❖ Bissanti seems particularly proud of the restaurant's slogan: "Which one are you?" It's written all over, including on the small menu card listing the four patties. ❖ The delicious little turkey burger (all patties are on the small side, each 5 ounces except the beef, which is 5 1/2 ) is made with Plainville Farms' hormone-free birds from upstate New York mixed with chopped apples, cooked, and topped with a mildly sweet cranberry chutney. Buns aren't exceptional; stale one night, soft and puffy another, both times buttered, griddled, and salted — though the food sorely lacks salt otherwise. ❖ The beef patty is shaped from Brandt Beef, a family-owned farm in California, and it has lots of good flavor. Like the other selections, this comes with a handful of waffle chips, thin and delicious one night, and then days later, too thick and no longer crisp.

❖ Salmon burger is a knockout, the roll spread with mayo, and the patty topped with a crisp fresh-tasting vinaigrette slaw. A side of fries ($2.50) shaped like shoestrings is just out of the deep-fat bath and wonderfully hot and good. Hand-cut sweet potato fries ($2.50) are very appealing. ❖ A mesclun salad ($3.50) with balsamic vinaigrette comes in a generous portion and every last leaf of these greens — my friend calls them "yuppie chow" — is bright and fresh. ❖ Only the veggie burger falls short. They're vegan, made by Blue Mango in Portland, Maine, and I guess they're an acquired taste — though the guacamole and tomato salsa garnishes are good. ❖ In its tall glass, a real chocolate milkshake ($5.50), made with Richardson's chocolate ice cream, whole milk, and sugar syrup, is thick, cold, intense, and seems like too much for one person. Minutes later, my husband is surprised to hear the unmistakable slurping the straw makes on the bottom of the glass when it's trying to draw up the last bits of liquid. And the giant homemade chocolate chipper ($1.50), with dark chocolate, isn't bad either.

❖ Citizen reviewers: See what you think.

SHERYL JULIAN, *Globe Staff*

# Jury Room

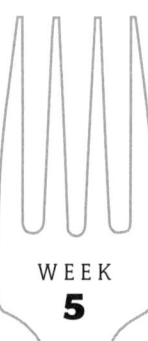

*39 Cottage Ave., Quincy*

*617-328-7234*

*www.thejuryroom.us*

*All major credit cards accepted. Wheelchair accessible.*

**PRICES** *$4.75-$27*
*(most bar menu items under $15).*

**HOURS** *Tue-Sat 4 p.m.-1 a.m.*

**ALCOHOL** *Full liquor license.*

WEEK 5

### HEY, TRY THESE

Steak cigars, crabmeat flatbread, Guilty as Charged chorizo flatbread, Petit Jury sliders, Parmesan crusted salmon, Courthouse ham, Heath bar bread pudding, ginger mascarpone cake, Key lime pie, orange creme brulee.

TASTING NOTES

---
---
---
---
---

BOSTON • CAMBRIDGE

**JUST DOWN THE STREET** from the Quincy District Courthouse, Jury Room capitalizes on the justice theme. ❖ The martinis ($9) have names like In terrorem, and Caveat emptor. Likewise the food, such as flatbreads ($7.50 to $9.50) named Court Appearance, Guilty as Charged, and Class Action. Sandwiches ($5.75 to $8.95) include Double Jeopardy, Beyond Reasonable Doubt Tuna Melt, and Power of Attorney. You get the idea. ❖ The chief justice behind all of this is Clint Smith, who has been in the restaurant business for years. For the Jury Room, he brought in chef Eileen O'Donoghue, formerly of — I'm not kidding — Jury's. ❖ Here's the thing about the Jury Room: You can eat on the cheap or you can splurge on a $27 steak. You can order off the restaurant menu if you're in the bar, and the bar menu if you're in the restaurant. ❖ Since we're Cheap Eaters both by occupation and preference, we order several things from the bar menu and some from the regular one. We start with steak cigars ($8), lean strips of beef wrapped in crispy phyllo pastry, and served with smoked Gouda sauce, reminiscent of a fancy Velveeta dip. The crunch, the smoke, the creamy finish offer a smorgasbord of sensations. ❖ A favorite is crabmeat flatbread ($9.50), a grilled saltine-type crust with a respectable helping of fresh crabmeat and melted goat cheese, accompanied by a caper aioli with bite. The Guilty as Charged ($9) flatbread is a tasty blend of chorizo, caramelized onions, and mozzarella. ❖ Petit Jury Sliders ($7.50) will make you sit bolt upright. Three mini buffalo chicken sandwiches are five-alarm. Though they're drizzled with blue cheese sauce, a small bowl of additional sauce would be welcome. ❖ Strawberry pecan salad ($5.50) is very fresh, but would have been better with candied pecans — and more of them. The only ordinary note is chicken tagliatelle diavolo ($15); the pasta lacks pizzazz and is a tad overdone. ❖ Desserts (all $6.50) are made on the premises and a delight. My friend George declares Heath bar bread pudding (with caramel sauce and vanilla ice cream) the best bread pudding he's ever had. Ginger mascarpone cake is a light, creamy alternative to standard cheesecake and comes with crumbled ginger snaps and mango coulis. ❖ Smith, who goes from table to table asking diners, "What's the verdict?" apologizes for the fact that the Key lime pie is warm, just recently baked. It's true that the flavor would have been more intense cool, but you know what? It's also wonderful just the way it is.

BELLA ENGLISH, *Globe Staff*

# La Siesta Restaurante

WEEK **6**

*70 Woodside Ave., Winthrop*
*617-846-2300*
*www.lasiestarestaurante.com*
*All major credit cards accepted.*
*Wheelchair accessible.*
**PRICES** *$2.50-$13.95.*
**HOURS** *Mon 5 p.m.-10 p.m., Tue-Sat 11:30 a.m.-10 p.m., Sun 4 p.m.-10 p.m.*
**ALCOHOL** *Full liquor license.*

### HEY, TRY THESE

Guacamole, fish tacos, tilapia Veracruz, enchiladas mole poblano, chicken poblano.

**TASTING NOTES**

BOSTON • CAMBRIDGE

"**THIS IS THE FOOD I GREW UP WITH,**" Martin Vasquez, co-owner of La Siesta Restaurante in Winthrop, explains enthusiastically. "I want to introduce people to it." ❖ The Mexican specialties Vasquez and his chef, Jacinto Pizarro, serve in La Siesta's sunny yellow dining room, really is the food their moms used to make. ❖ You're certainly not going to find salsa and guacamole this good elsewhere. The salsa is full of ripe tomato flavor, with chunks of tomato and bits of cilantro kicked up a notch by jalapeno peppers. It's tempting to make a meal out of the guacamole ($6.95 for a bowl). The cool, smooth puree is studded with generous chunks of rich, ripe avocado and bits of tomato. A dash of jalapeño gives it a little kick. ❖ Fish tacos ($13.95 for three) are soft tortillas filled with grilled tilapia, pico de gallo, and a chipotle cream sauce. The many hunks of fish are tender and taste of the grill — a nice contrast with the spicy mayonnaise. ❖ Though the menu lists one of the enchilada choices as "mole poblano" ($8.95), Vasquez explains that it's not exactly mole. "I call it mole so people will know that the sauce is sweet," Vasquez explains. Two soft corn tortillas are wrapped around juicy hunks of chicken and topped with the dark sauce made from dried poblano peppers slow-cooked with Mexican chocolate, cinnamon, sugar, and sesame seeds. Its big, rich flavor goes nicely with the chicken. ❖ Tilapia Veracruz ($13.95) is a piece of fish sautéed with white wine, lemon, olives, mushrooms, onions, and tomatoes. The fish is moist and perfectly cooked and comes with a generous serving of rice. It's a lovely dish. ❖ In a sort of Mexican take on chicken marsala, a roasted poblano cream sauce with mushrooms covers white and dark meat in the chicken poblano ($13.95). The sauce is slightly sweet and earthy. ❖ An enormous chile verde burrito ($9.95) is filled with marinated pork and covered with a tomatillo sauce. The green sauce is bright and flavorful, but there's a lot of salt in the pork, and after several bites it becomes overpowering. ❖ For dessert, La Siesta offers fried ice cream, flan, and apple burrito ($3.95 each). We try the flan, and even though the custard has a nice flavor, the consistency is way off. It had been cooked too long, and is tough to cut. ❖ We don't mind. We're all full, the service is polite and friendly, and the dining room, with its pretty tables and colorful chairs, has a distinct south of the border feel.

ANN LUISA CORTISSOZ, *Globe Staff*

SOMERVILLE • BEYOND

# Viva Mi Arepa

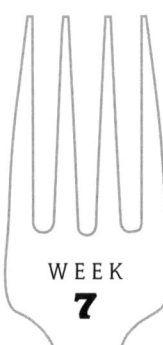

5197 Washington St., West Roxbury
617-323-7844
www.spitfiresbbq.com
MasterCard and Visa accepted.
Entrance wheelchair accessible; bathroom not accessible.
**PRICES** Appetizers: $2.25-$7. Entrees: $7-$17.50. Desserts: $2.50-$3.
**HOURS** Tue-Sat 11 a.m.-10 p.m., Sun 11 a.m.-7 p.m.
**ALCOHOL** None.

WEEK 7

## HEY, TRY THESE

Arepas with white cheese, chicken, or pork; stewed chicken, beef, or pork; grilled chicken, fried pork chops, red snapper in coconut sauce, garlic shrimp, paella (order 24 hours in advance), flan, fruit shakes.

TASTING NOTES
_____
_____
_____
_____
_____

BOSTON · CAMBRIDGE

**VIVA MI AREPA MAY SEAT ONLY 12,** it's out-of-the-way on a somewhat drab West Roxbury corner, and so do-it-yourself that you order at a counter, and then peer at specials in steamer trays through a scratched, yellowed window. Oh, and it's loud (the TV, and sometimes the radio as well, is always on). But what you trade in the usual niceties, you gain in good, hard-to-find Venezuelan cooking. ❖ Once there, your first words should be "I'd like an arepa, please." Chef and owner Edner Trentetun makes his arepas fresh to order with Harina P.A.N. cornmeal, which has a subtle corn flavor like that of grits. They take about 20 minutes to grill, which we preferred to having them fried. Pressed down with white farmer's cheese oozing out, the queso blanco arepa ($4) is as comforting as the best mom-made grilled cheese. With their garlicky, wine-spiked tomato sauce sopped up into the bread, pulled chicken ($4) and pork ($4) arepas have just the right tang. ❖ During the day, homemade cornmeal empanadas ($2.25) fly out the door. Or try cachapas ($6-$7), savory corn pancakes with sweet whole corn kernels, meat, and cheese grilled right into the dough. ❖ The hopping lunchtime crowd also tends to favor the day's "dinners" ($7-$9). We enjoyed the tomato-y carne guisada (stewed beef), herb-crusted pollo asado (grilled chicken), and lemony pernil guisado (stewed pork), as much as the savory red beans, fluffy white rice, sweet-and-juicy fried plantains, and wonderfully soft, juice-box-size hunks of steamed yucca. ❖ Evenings are quieter. While a few stragglers come in for take-out, we're the only table in the cheery space. The a la carte entrees we try deserve a greater draw. ❖ Whole red snapper ($12) with its rich coconut sauce, moist flesh, fat green olives, and surprise smear of avocado-cilantro-garlic paste, could easily win applause at an upscale hot spot, although the bones might distract some diners. ❖ We had ordered paella 24 hours in advance ($15-$17.50) and were glad we did. Every piece of seafood — from the squid and calamari to the shrimp, mussels, and littleneck clams — is tender and plump. ❖ Nearly every dish (especially the pork chops, $9) is even better with a squirt of garlicky "guasacaca," an addictive avocado-parsley mayo (25 cents). Though perhaps desserts should be eaten without it. Try sweet, eggy flan ($2.50) or a tropical fruit shake ($3). ❖ To dine on Trentetun's cooking, you need to be willing to suffer through a blaring TV with programs like "Make Me a Supermodel." And yes we would — even if they turned up the volume.

DENISE TAYLOR, *Globe Correspondent*

# Shiraz Cuisine

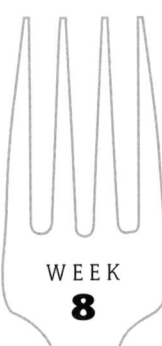

WEEK **8**

72 Bigelow Ave., Watertown
617-923-2222
www.theshirazcuisine.com
All major credit cards accepted.
Wheelchair accessible.
**PRICES** Appetizers, soups, and salads: $3.50-$5.99. Entrees: $9.99-$15.99 (one combo platter $20.99). Desserts: $4.99.
**HOURS** Mon-Thu 11:30 a.m.-10 p.m. Fri-Sun 11:30 a.m.-10:30 p.m.
**ALCOHOL** Beer and wine.

## HEY, TRY THESE

Eggplant topped with mint, yogurt with chopped cucumber and mint, stuffed grape leaves, Shirazi salad, Olivieh salad, chicken kubideh (skewered ground kabob), shish kabob, lamb shank.

**TASTING NOTES**
_____
_____
_____
_____

BOSTON • CAMBRIDGE

**THE PERSIAN COMMUNITY** has discovered Shiraz Cuisine. This restaurant was opened by Moe and Parisa Anbardar, who used to own Cafe Habibi, an eight-seat spot in Allston. Now the couple, both from Tehran, are offering the dishes of their native Iran in a stylish spot with small blue pendants over sleek tables and white cloths forming waves against a back-lit blue ceiling. ❖ In its geographical spot between the Far East and the Middle East, Iran seems to share tastes and flavors with many regions. Dark and aromatic eggplant, for instance, in a dish called kashk o bademjan ($5.99), is grilled and pureed, then mixed with fried onions and covered with a minty yogurt sauce. It has the smoky quality of other eggplant purees, but the sweetness of the vegetables is offset by slightly sour homemade yogurt. Another familiar dish is Olivieh salad ($5.99), made from diced chicken breast mixed with mayonnaise, chopped eggs, potatoes, and peas. Pickles add a piquant taste. ❖ Other dishes have a little acidic bite. All entrees come with barley soup ($4.25 without entree), which includes lots of lemon juice and tomato paste simmered for many hours until the pot thickens from the grains. "House dough," an ancient drink of thick, carbonated lemony yogurt ($2.50), is a sour slurp that's an acquired taste. ❖ Kabobs such as boneless lamb ($15.99) or shish kabob with lamb ($15.99) are arranged with the meat on one side of the plate, a heap of rice beside it, along with lemon wedges and grilled vegetables. Boneless lamb is in a lightly spicy tomato-flavored sauce; shish kabob is simply tender chunks of leg meat with caramelized edges. ❖ Parisa Anbardar, who runs the front of the house, explains that her husband is cooking with his brother, Amir. They brought a gas grill from home, along with a machine to make chicken kubideh ($10.99), a skewer of ground poultry flavored with saffron and grilled just to the point that it's quite moist. When a customer wants kubideh, they grind the meat to order. ❖ Persian ice cream ($4.99) is homemade from cream, pistachios, saffron, and rose water, but other desserts come from Watertown's Tabrizi Bakery, which specializes in Persian confections, including large triangles of nutty bagh lava ($4.99) — say it fast and you'll recognize what it is — and roulette ($4.99), a kind of jelly roll with creamy filling. You should usually skip dessert at restaurants where they're not made on the premises, but the marriage of Shiraz and Tabrizi seems to be a particularly good one.

SHERYL JULIAN, *Globe Staff*

# Tom Yum Koong Thai

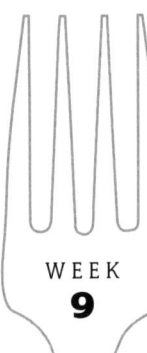

WEEK **9**

*11 Forest St., Medford*
*781-393-0888*
*www.tomyumkoong.net*
*Visa and MasterCard accepted.*
*Wheelchair accessible.*
**PRICES** *$3.95-$15.95.*
**HOURS** *Daily 10:30 a.m.-11 p.m.*
**ALCOHOL** *None.*

### HEY, TRY THESE

Tom yum soup, shumai, crispy chicken basil, scallop bamboo, spicy eggplant, massaman curry, fried bananas, sweet sticky rice with Thai custard.

**TASTING NOTES**

*BOSTON • CAMBRIDGE*

"**NEXT TIME, PLEASE COME IN AND SIT,**" Tom Daranuwat tells a customer who is picking up a takeout order from Daranuwat's Medford Square restaurant, Tom Yum Koong Thai Cuisine. Daranuwat has been saying this a lot lately.

❖ While it didn't take area residents long to figure out that Tom Yum Koong was a great place to get Thai takeout when it opened, it has taken customers a while to realize that the little storefront has expanded into a bright, cheerful, 38-seat dining room. That's a shame, because the food at Tom Yum Koong, made by Daranuwat's wife, Siriwan, is even better when eaten right where it's made. ❖ The Daranuwats are from Bangkok, where Siriwan learned to cook, but she never prepared food professionally until they came to the United States.

❖ Siriwan's version of traditional tom yum soup ($3.50) is a clear broth with shrimp that is perfectly balanced between spicy and sour. ❖ Steamed shumai ($5.95 for six) are tender little dumplings bursting with shrimp and chicken. And little wonder why crispy chicken basil ($10.95) is Tom Yum Koong's most popular dish. Chunks of chicken are battered and deep-fried until they're golden outside but still juicy inside and served with fried basil leaves that add a bright burst of flavor. Spicy eggplant with tofu ($9.95) boasts thick slices of the vegetable, first deep-fried, then stir-fried in a chili sauce and served with meaty browned tofu. The earthy eggplant flavor is a great complement to the spicy chili. ❖ Various curries — avocado, black pepper mango, and yellow — can be ordered with beef, chicken, tofu, duck, or seafood. Massaman curry with chicken ($9.95) is a lovely rendition of the southern Thai dish, with carrots, sweet potato, and chunks of the bird in a curry that's sweet from coconut milk balanced by layers of spicy flavor. ❖ Portions at Tom Yum Koong are generous, but no matter how full you are, don't miss dessert. Fried bananas ($3.95) are a satisfying combination of softness and crunch, with sweet, ripe yellow fruit and shreds of coconut wrapped in egg roll wrappers and deep-fried. They get top billing until we try sweet sticky rice with Thai custard ($5.95), a favorite in Thailand. ❖ Tom Yum Koong delivers to Medford, Somerville, Malden, Arlington, Melrose, Stoneham, and parts of Cambridge, Winchester, and Charlestown. But the best way to satisfy a craving for Thai food is to take a seat at the restaurant and let Siriwan Daranuwat send her specialties from the kitchen to your table. It'll make Tom Daranuwat's day.

ANN LUISA CORTISSOZ, *Globe Staff*

# Dino's

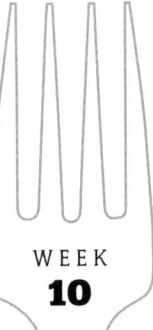

WEEK **10**

*141 Salem St., North End, Boston*
*617-227-1991*
*All major credit cards accepted.*
*Not wheelchair accessible (one step up).*
*No restroom.*
**PRICES** *$8-$16.95.*
**HOURS** *11 a.m.-10 p.m. daily.*
**ALCOHOL** *Beer and wine.*

### HEY, TRY THESE

Chicken, ziti, and broccoli in garlic-white wine sauce; veal Parmesan; chicken marsala; anything with pesto.

**TASTING NOTES**

BOSTON • CAMBRIDGE

**GOOD FOOD IS WONDERFUL.** Good, inexpensive food is even better. That's why I often find myself at Dino's when I'm in the North End and don't want to drop big bucks on dinner. ❖ Nearly a decade old, Dino's is basically a glorified sub shop, which means that besides selling comically oversize sandwiches (made on 16-inch French loaves), it also serves lobster ravioli, sausage cacciatore, frutti di mare, and a wide variety of other meat and pasta dishes. ❖ Dino's isn't fancy. There's no table service or even a restroom, decor is minimal, and on cool nights, tables sometimes get blasted with chilly air as the door opens and closes. But the food arrives quickly, ingredients are fresh, portions are generous, and prices won't take your breath away. Most pastas are around $10, and you can order beer or wine with your meal. In other words, it's the quintessential cheap-eats destination. ❖ Mohaj Shaban, who owns Dino's with his wife, Ann, is a sweetheart. Warm and gregarious, he truly seems to want his customers to enjoy their meals, and he accommodates nearly any special request.
❖ My favorite foods here are the simplest ones. The pastas can be made with a choice of sauces: marinara, pink cream, pesto, pesto cream, or scampi. But a trio of garlic, white wine, and olive oil is also an option, and tastes divine with chicken, ziti, and broccoli ($11) or the ravioli, gnocchi, and tortellini dishes. The lightness of the sauce lets the flavor of the pasta fillings, including cheese, spinach, and pumpkin, shine through. Sweet chicken marsala ($12.95) with meaty mushrooms and salty capicola is also a success. So is tender veal Parmesan ($11.95), although eggplant parm ($10.95) is oddly watery and fairly bland. ❖ Fresh shellfish rim a plate of spaghetti and clams ($13.95), but the mixture would have deeper flavor if clams were also blended into the sauce. Baked fettuccini ($11.95) isn't what we expect; instead of a crusty, oven-browned casserole, it's a heap of noodles in heavy cream sauce that coagulates quickly and unappetizingly. It's mixed with chunks of chicken that are nicely tenderized by the cream, but this dish looks like a heart attack on a plate. ❖ Once again, lighter is better, like the gorgeously green chicken pesto or Dino's chicken sandwiches ($8) topped with balsamic-glazed portobello mushrooms and roasted plum tomatoes. You certainly get your money's worth: A full foot long, they're so eye-poppingly big that even the linebacker-size customer at the next table looks awestruck as he prepares to dig in.

SACHA PFEIFFER, *Globe Staff*

# Machu Picchu
## Charcoal Chicken & Grill

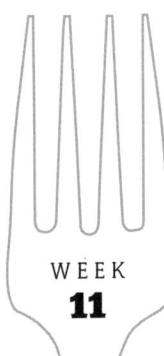

WEEK **11**

25 Union Square, Somerville
617-623-7972
www.machupicchuboston.com
All major credit cards accepted.
Wheelchair accessible.

**PRICES** Appetizers: $4-$13. Entrees: $6-$14. Desserts: $3.50-$6.50.

**HOURS** Mon-Thu 11:30 a.m.-10 p.m., Fri-Sat 11:30 a.m.-10:30 p.m., Sun 11 a.m.-10 p.m.

**ALCOHOL** Beer and wine.

### HEY, TRY THESE

Choclo Peruano (Peruvian corn and cheese), fried yucca, roasted pork tamale, rotisserie chicken with misky salad, chicken parrillero sandwich, el Peruanisimo sandwich (roast pork and sweet potato), tres leches cake, leche asada custard.

TASTING NOTES

BOSTON • CAMBRIDGE

**THE MAGIC NUMBER AT** Machu Picchu Charcoal Chicken & Grill is 24. That's how many hours their rotisserie chicken soaks in a secret brew before it's slid onto a spit and roasted over hot coals to a succulent, smoky-to-the-bone perfection. ❖ Twenty-four is also about the number of seconds that it takes to walk to Rosy and Hugo Cerna's other restaurant, also dubbed Machu Picchu. Why open a second Peruvian restaurant a tamale's throw from the first? ❖ "Because we really wanted to serve pollos a la brasa," says Rosy Cerna about their charcoal chicken. "It's a national dish in Peru, but... pollos a la brasa has to have a restaurant of its own." ❖ And now it does. In a storefront in Somerville's Union Square, behind the comfy dining room, a special Peruvian rotisserie oven hulks in the kitchen. In it golden brown birds prickling with cumin, oregano — and other spices Cerna won't reveal — turn and turn over hardwood coals. ❖ We order the quarter chicken with misky salad ($5.99) and the plate our attentive server brings us is a carbophobe's delight. Our juicy, beer-marinated chicken breast comes shored up by a green salad topped by a produce shelf's worth of steamed veggies and a generous fan of sliced avocado. For a full dinner, it's a bargain. ❖ The hits don't end with the rotisserie meals. Machu No. 2 turns out nice starters, sandwiches, salads, and other grilled meats. Try the fabulous, nearly paperback-book-size tamale ($6.99). Tender roast pork, boiled egg, and tangy olive are tucked into a cornmeal dough so comforting, it's no wonder it's breakfast in Peru. ❖ Choclo Peruano, Peruvian corn ($6.99), arrives looking like giant, mutant corn on the cob. Its kernels are plucked from the cob and nibbled with firm, white cubes of fresh farmers cheese. Together, they satisfy in the quiet way that good bread with fresh mozzarella does. ❖ Try the el Peruanisimo, roast pork and sweet potato sandwich ($5.99), which layers a party's worth of flavors onto a lovely, light toasted bun. The secret is hot aji slices, cilantro, and tangy lime-based Peruvian salsa. Chicken parrillero ($5.99) deserves a ribbon for taking the usual dull, dry grilled bird and turning it into a flavorful, juicy sandwich. ❖ Desserts deftly hit the usual creamy notes with leche asada, baked custard; wonderfully rich "three milk" tres leches cake; and rice pudding fragrant with orange ($3.50 each). Or walk a half block and finish up at Machu No. 1 with a frothy pisco sour cocktail. They certainly make it easy to visit both.

DENISE TAYLOR, *Globe Correspondent*

# Esperia Grill & Rotisserie

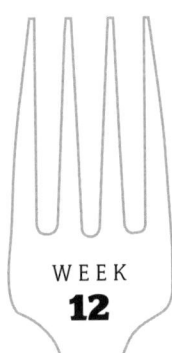

WEEK **12**

344 Washington St., Brighton Center
617-254-8337
www.esperiagrill.com
All major credit cards accepted.
Wheelchair accessible.

**PRICES** Appetizers: $2.95-$6.95. Salads, sandwiches, pizzas: $4.75-$15.95. Entrees: $5.95-$14.95. Desserts: $2.50-$2.75.

**HOURS** Mon-Sat 11 a.m.-10 p.m., Sun noon-10 p.m.

**ALCOHOL** Wine and beer.

### HEY, TRY THESE

Taramosalata, eggplant salad, gyro dinner, chicken kabob, Greek-style roast potatoes, string beans, galaktobouriko, koulourakia.

TASTING NOTES

**FOR 20 YEARS,** Efthymios (Tim) and Georgia Athanasiadis ran Center House of Pizza in Brighton Center. Then they turned the place inside out, renamed it Esperia Grill & Rotisserie, and reopened as an authentic Greek kouzina. It sits back from the main street, tucked beside a Dunkin' Donuts. ❖ "The way we cook here," says Tim, "that's the way we cook at home."
❖ Esperia does a brisk take-out business, some from neighboring St. Elizabeth's Hospital; the local Greek community comes for specialties like taramosalata, the creamy pink spread made from red caviar and potato, and eggplant salad, a garlicky puree with vinegar and roasted peppers (both $4.50 for a half-pint; $6.50 for a pint). ❖ Customers order at a counter, then sit down; if you stay, someone brings your meal. Tim keeps a careful eye on the room. That's not to say that you get your food in minutes. Georgia may be baking something to order, as she did my spanakopita one night ($4.95 as an appetizer). Instead of layering phyllo dough in a deep pan and cutting the large rectangle into squares, she had made an individual envelope wrapped around a creamy feta and spinach filling, which made four flaky edges. Yes, I had to wait, but so much good cooking isn't fast — it can't be and shouldn't be.
❖ No one here skimps on garlic or salt. Georgia's moussaka ($11.95), with spicy ground beef, is topped with a puffy, eggy white sauce. Juicy chicken kabobs come in pairs (two skewers for $11.95), and with them you get a salad and two sides. Don't miss Greek-style potatoes, cooked in plenty of oil, lemon, and wild oregano from home. ❖ Gyros (pronounced "year-o") is made with pork or chicken carved off a vertical rotisserie ($11.95 for the dinner). The highly seasoned pork, almost too salty for us, comes on a thick, handmade pita that has no pocket, along with the garlic-yogurt sauce, tzatziki, and a tomato and onion salad. ❖ The Athanasiadises are constantly in motion and go at it seven days a week. She says, "We're not afraid of hard work." They probably don't know that the glass cruets of oil and vinegar on the table, a nice touch, are very sticky by the end of the day. But you forget quickly when you bite into Georgia's heavenly galaktobourika, sweet custard wrapped inside rectangles of golden phyllo, or her brilliant koulourakia, buttery, lightly sweetened cookies with the texture of shortbread and the shape of mini doughnuts. Forget the neighboring coffee place. This is what doughnuts should taste like.

SHERYL JULIAN, *Globe Staff*

# Original Kelly's Landing

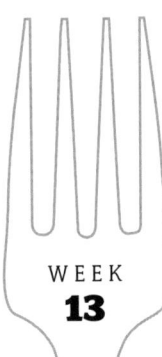

**WEEK 13**

81 L St., South Boston
617-268-8900
www.theoriginalkellys.com
All major credit cards accepted. Fully accessible.
**PRICES** $1.99-$19.99.
**HOURS** Sun noon-9 p.m.,
Mon-Thu 11:30 a.m.-9 p.m.,
Fri-Sat 11:30 a.m.-10 p.m.
**ALCOHOL** Beer, wine, cordials.

## HEY, TRY THESE

Turkey tips, sirloin tips, turkey dinner, fried clams, fish and chips, baked scallops, grilled salmon.

**TASTING NOTES**

**FOR DECADES,** Kelly's and Southie went hand in hand. Opened in 1927, Kelly's Landing was a beloved South Boston clam shack. When the state bulldozed the dilapidated place in 1997, it seemed the poignant end of an era. ❖ But in 2004, Dick Kelly, the grandson of the founders of Kelly's Landing, resurrected his family's restaurant not far from its original site. And look at the one-time snack bar now! The Original Kelly's Landing boasts a 50-seat dining room, a small bar, a bistro feel, and a menu that stretches well beyond seafood. ❖ Kelly's is still a clam joint at heart, though, priding itself on generous portions, good value, family-friendly dining (kiddie meals cost $3.99), waitresses who know the locals, and decent, low-frills food. ❖ There's something for everyone here: Reubens, club sandwiches, tuna melts, burgers, pasta, meatloaf, chicken parm. Daily specials are pure Yankee: chicken pot pie, boiled dinners, pot roast. The homemade soups ("no cans allowed!" the menu pledges) are extremely good, especially chunky tomato-rice, creamy chicken stew, and beef-barley made with delicious leftover prime rib or roast beef (cup $1.99, bowl $2.99). ❖ Kelly's makes the finest turkey tips and sirloin tips I've had ($10.99/$11.99, combo $13.99). They're moist, robustly marinated, and cooked exactly to order. The turkey dinner ($9.99, all white meat $1 more), with squash, mashed potatoes, cranberry sauce, and stuffing, is excellent; the kitchen roasts a 30-pound turkey nearly every day. ❖ Skip the pastas: Chicken broccoli ziti ($9.99) was skimpy on broccoli and overloaded with heavily breaded chicken chunks, while veal marsala ($11.99) atop rice was strangely soupy. ❖ But let's get real. You go to Kelly's for seafood, and for that I have only praise. The delectable fried clams are coated with a mixture of corn and white flour that's frequently sifted, and cooked in oil that's changed often, leaving them virtually greaseless. The heaping fish and chips could possibly feed three, and a crispy version is battered with Japanese panko bread crumbs. Baked scrod ($10.99, $9.99 Fridays before 4 p.m.) and baked scallops ($16.99) come with a buttery topping of seasoned bread crumbs and white wine. ❖ Grilled salmon ($13.99) is a pleasure, and I was stunned to learn it's previously frozen; I would have sworn it was fresh. The crab cakes ($5.99), one of the few items not made in-house, are so-so, weirdly smooth and drowned in runny lobster bisque. ❖ Two more homemade standouts: sweet pickle tartar sauce and coleslaw seasoned with dill seed, just a dab of mayo, and a dash of sugar.

SACHA PFEIFFER, *Globe Staff*

# The Four's

WEEK **14**

*15 Cottage Ave., Quincy*
*617-471-4447*
*www.thefours.com*
*All major credit cards accepted.*
*Wheelchair accessible.*
**PRICES** *$3.50-$19.95.*
**HOURS** *Daily 11 a.m.-1 a.m.*
**ALCOHOL** *Full license.*

### HEY, TRY THESE

Four's Triple Play, burgers, pizza, ice cream sundae.

**TASTING NOTES**
_____
_____
_____
_____
_____

BOSTON • CAMBRIDGE

**WE KNEW THAT THE FOUR'S** at North Station had been named the number one sports bar in America by Sports Illustrated in 2005, mainly because of its proximity to what was then the FleetCenter. We wanted to check out The Four's country cousin in Quincy. Would the sporty atmosphere transfer to a place that's sort of hidden away in a parking lot area near the district courthouse? ❖ Yes, and no. ❖ You can tell it's a sports bar from the moment you pull open the brass door handles — shaped like baseball bats — at the entrance. But whenever I've been in other sports bars, I haven't escaped without having beer sloshed on me or being forced to listen to a steady stream of swears unleashed by passionate Boston fans. ❖ At the Quincy Four's, named in honor of Bobby Orr's jersey number, we watch both the Red Sox and the Bruins play on the requisite bank of television screens. ❖ This is a sports bar with class, if you'll pardon the oxymoron. From the mural of the Harvard-Yale crew teams on the Charles River to the blackened swordfish and shrimp Diane, this isn't your typical joint. It's a pretty place, dominated by a long polished bar. Sports memorabilia gives it the feel of an informal museum, with oars, vintage photos, hockey sticks. ❖ We start with the appetizer special, shrimp sauté ($10.95), which is half a dozen plump shrimp in a garlicky wine sauce, served with chunks of chewy, crisp focaccia. ❖ We like our carbs straight up, so we order the Four's Triple Play ($9.95) — a platter of jalapeño poppers, potato skins, and buffalo chicken fingers. The potato skins are a tad dry, but the chicken fingers are moist and fiery. Even the pizza here is upscale, with a thin crust, small slices of fresh tomato, and a scattering of fresh basil. Try the scallop and bacon ($15.95), with an abundance of bay scallops, a nice combination of sweet and smoky flavors. ❖ The Four's burger ($8.95) is a half-pound patty, flavorful, cooked just right, and topped with cheese, caramelized onions, peppers, and mushrooms. It comes with baked beans, pickle, and a choice of steak fries or pasta salad. ❖ For dessert, the ice cream sundae ($4.95), a creamy concoction, is loaded with good stuff. The ordinary cheesecake ($6.50) is overpriced. ❖ The gentleman at our table reports that one of the day's sports pages hangs above the urinals in the men's room, framed and presumably changed daily. Hmmm. Maybe The Four's, Quincy branch, is a real sports bar after all.

BELLA ENGLISH, *Globe Staff*

# Sophia's Cafe

*141 Dorchester Ave., South Boston
(at the Macallen Building)*

*617-426-1115*

*www.sophiascafe.com*

*All major credit cards accepted.
Wheelchair accessible.*

**PRICES** *$3-$9.
Lunch specials: $5.25-$7.95.*

**HOURS** *Mon-Fri 6:30 a.m.-6 p.m.,
Sat 8 a.m.-5 p.m., Sun 8 a.m.-3 p.m.*

**ALCOHOL** *None.*

WEEK 15

### HEY, TRY THESE

Happy Goat, Apple of My Eye, chicken pesto pressed sandwich, chili, brownies, muffins.

TASTING NOTES

**AS SALES MANAGER** for the eco-chic Macallen and next-door Court Square Press condo projects in Southie, Dominique Lange saw a business opportunity. "I knew there was a need for something beyond a pub on the corner," said Lange, explaining why he and his wife, Jennifer, opened Sophia's Cafe on the street level of the Macallen Building. ❖ Sophia's is a simple place with admirable ambitions. The menu gets no fancier than soups, salads, sandwiches, baked goods, and coffee. Neither Jennifer, Dominique, nor his brother, Sebastian, who helps run the place, are trained cooks, but they put a lot of love in their food. ❖ Jennifer makes most of the pastries and Sebastian makes most of the soups. There are a surprising number of homemade items, even though the Langes could easily rely on suppliers. Sophia's serves two of my favorite local chilis: one with ground chicken, kidney beans, cilantro, and sweet corn, the other with ground turkey, white beans, green chilies, and a hint of cinnamon. Both are thick, meaty, and well-seasoned. ❖ From the pastry case, the deeply fudgy brownies (secret ingredient: coffee) are especially good, and I also like the pudgy muffins (banana, blueberry, or raisin bran), which have soft centers and crusty tops. Lemon squares are a touch gummy, and the chocolate bread pudding, made from leftover chocolate croissants, is a doughy dud. ❖ In keeping with current fashion, pressed sandwiches are offered, too. Especially good are two cold sandwiches: the Happy Goat ($8), with chicken, goat cheese, mixed greens, and oily sun-dried tomatoes that soak deliciously into the bread, and the Apple of My Eye ($7), a ham-and-Swiss elevated by Dijon mustard, multigrain bread studded with golden raisins, and apple slaw jazzed up with mint and jalapeño. But thumbs-down to the Mediterranean wrap ($7), which is drowning in hummus and skimpy on veggies. ❖ Warning: service can be poky, and the specials often look like the handiwork of a kindergartener, like the "pizza" (also called "bruschetta" or "pizza bruschetta," depending on the day) that's little more than dry toast with a dollop of tomatoes. ❖ Most of all, Sophia's needs to embrace its inner cutesiness. The specials chalkboard is a cozy accent, but it would look nicer without the chicken-scratch handwriting and erase marks, and the pastry case would be more alluring if it weren't often so bare and disheveled. Still, it's hard not to root for a little place like this, which has so many homespun touches. And once all those surrounding condos are finally occupied, those exquisite brownies are going to be in serious demand.

SACHA PFEIFFER, *Globe Staff*

# Pho and Thai

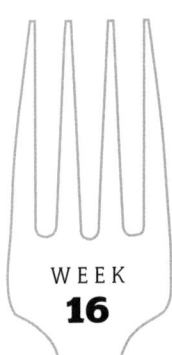

WEEK **16**

63 White St., Waverly Square, Belmont
617-484-1118
www.phoandthai.com
MasterCard and Visa accepted.
Wheelchair accessible.

**PRICES** *Appetizers, soups, salads: $4.95-$11.95. Noodles, rice dishes, curries, entrees: $7.95-$17.95.*

**HOURS** *Mon-Fri lunch 11:30 a.m.-3:30 p.m., dinner 4:30-10 p.m., Sat-Sun lunch noon-3:30 p.m., dinner 4:30-10 p.m.*

**ALCOHOL** *Beer and wine.*

### HEY, TRY THESE

Green papaya salad, tiger's tear salad, steamed tofu bun, pad see eaw, kra-pow with beef.

TASTING NOTES

BOSTON • CAMBRIDGE

**THE THREE THAI PARTNERS** who opened Pho and Thai in Belmont's Waverly Square — Sasirat Wyckoff, Tusnee Wutimongkolchai, and Aporn Vongsavat — probably had no idea that whatever they did would be compared to Patou Thai in Belmont Center, a restaurant about a mile away. The stunning Patou sets the standard not just for Thai cuisine, but for graciousness and service. ❖ Pho and Thai is mostly Thai, though Vongsavat, who established the menu and does the cooking, feels confident in Vietnamese, Malaysian, and Korean cuisines. Thai food is more expensive than Vietnamese, she says, and the economy is down. So to a classic Thai menu she offers several bowls of pho, the big-flavored Vietnamese soup, and the traditional bun, made with rice vermicelli noodles and a mound of fresh mint, peanuts, and bean sprouts. ❖ Alas, this isn't Patou, but you can eat well and enjoy Vongsavat's take on many familiar dishes. Satay, the classic skewers of marinated beef or chicken with peanut sauce ($5.95), is made with thin, well-flavored beef one night, and long lumps of tasteless chicken another. Steamed shumai, filled with vegetables ($5.95), come in very tender dumpling wrappers. Edamame ($4.95) are hot and plump. ❖ Irresistibly crunchy green papaya salad ($8.95) is delicious, though the shrimp are gummy. Tiger's tear salad ($11.95) is the outstanding appetizer here, with luscious strips of rare sirloin in a spicy sauce, accompanied by cool greens. ❖ Pho ga, or chicken soup ($7.95), is a good bowl but without the depth of a pho ladled out in a Vietnamese restaurant. Pho beef meatball ($7.95) comes with slices of a dense meat with the texture of tongue. The classic Vietnamese vermicelli salads called bun also don't seem authentic, though they're very good. Vongsavat's steamed tofu, in large squares, is remarkable. ❖ Crispy pad Thai looks like crumbles of shredded wheat and tastes wonderful in its rich mixture of egg, bean sprouts, and peanuts. The star of the pad dishes is pad see eaw with wide rice noodles. All the pad variations come in chicken, tofu, or beef ($9.95) or shrimp or seafood ($10.95). ❖ Kra-pow ($11.95), another outstanding entree, is a mixture of spicy ground beef (you can also order chicken) with onions, green peppers, and mushrooms.
❖ Vongsavat opened Sweet Lemons in Weymouth half a dozen years ago and keeps an eye on what her customers are ordering. So she's bound to smooth out the little things. Then she'll no longer be compared to Patou Thai. Pho and Thai will be another option on the growing landscape.

SHERYL JULIAN, *Globe Staff*

# Z Square in the Park

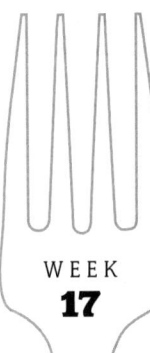

*Zero Post Office Square, Boston*
*617-728-0101, www.z-square.com*
*All major credit cards accepted.*
*Wheelchair accessible.*

**PRICES** *$4-$17.*

**HOURS** *Tue-Thu 7 a.m.-9 p.m., Fri-Sat 7 a.m.-10 p.m., Sun 7 a.m.-3 p.m., Mon closed.*

WEEK **17**

## The Carving Station

*1 Beacon St, Boston*
*617-367-8500, www.thecarvingstation.com*
*All major credit cards accepted.*
*Wheelchair accessible.*

**PRICES** *Sandwiches: $7.25-$7.95. Salads: $6.*

**HOURS** *Mon-Fri 11 a.m.-3 p.m.*

### HEY, TRY THESE

Panini specials, Mediterranean tuna sandwich, chacarero sandwich. Ham and egg sandwich, Reuben sandwich, roast chicken sandwich.

TASTING NOTES

BOSTON • CAMBRIDGE

**IF THERE'S ANYTHING A DOWNTOWN** lunch spot requires for success, it's a smooth operation. A lunch break is only so long. The third location of the Z Square chain (the others are in Harvard and Kenmore squares), Z serves a small-but-growing menu of sandwiches, panini, soups, and salads. It's the kind of food owner David Zebny says he wanted to eat during his 15-year tenure working in Post Office Square. ❖ Despite many tasty items on the menu, the new spot hasn't yet figured out how to efficiently move customers in and out. Striking white tiles and a counter-in-the-round look beautiful but set the stage for some disorganized lunchtime drama. ❖ Good choices are the daily pressed sandwiches ($7), whose fillings rotate throughout the week. Goat cheese and roasted vegetable ($6.50) has a great balance of meltiness, tang, and texture; a pressed muffaletta ($7.50), with mortadella, salami, provolone, and olive salad spread, is a rich, savory delight. ❖ Also good are Mediterranean tuna ($8) on multigrain bread and Z Square's take on a chacarero ($9), the Chilean sandwich popularized by the Downtown Crossing take-out spot. Piled on a soft roll, sliced flank steak, green beans, avocado, Jack cheese, and chimichurri sauce are a killer combo. ❖ In terms of moving people along, Z Square should look to the Carving Station for ideas. This deli, which specializes in hand-carved meats, gets good food to you promptly, a lesson owner Laurence Wintersteen says he learned from running nearby Pressed Sandwiches. ❖ The Carving Station is a solid concept. Meats are roasted in-house and carved to order, and sides like mac and cheese, potato salad, and baked beans are made from scratch. Even the chips, seasoned and baked tortilla triangles, are homemade — and addictive. But there are a few disappointments. Our lunch group is excited by the prospect of pulled pork, but the meat is too sweet and flabby. In a subsequent visit, we stick to the basics: tasty roast chicken ($7.50) and the Reuben ($7.50), with layers of thinly sliced corned beef and a judicious application of Russian dressing. ❖ If the Carving Station scaled its long menu back a bit, it could focus on stand-out items like the ham and egg sandwich ($7.50), in which thick slabs of ham are stacked with hard-cooked eggs, cheese, and a lively yellow pepper ketchup on a puffy wheat bun. ❖ The Carving Station and Z Square are both welcome additions to a humdrum downtown lunch scene. With a few tweaks to the menu (Carving Station) and service (Z Square), both could earn their midday lines.

LEIGH BELANGER , *Globe Correspondent*

# 303 Cafe

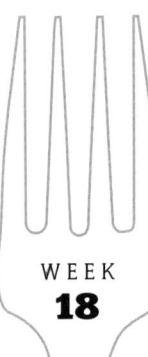

WEEK **18**

*303 Sumner St., East Boston*
*617-569-3001*
*www.303cafe.com*
*All major credit cards accepted.*
*Wheelchair accessible.*

**PRICES** *Breakfast: $4-$11. Lunch: $6-$10.50. Dinner: $7-$17.*

**HOURS** *Tue-Thu 7 a.m.-9 p.m., Fri-Sat 7 a.m.-10 p.m., Sun 7 a.m.-3 p.m., Mon closed.*

**ALCOHOL** *Beer and wine.*

### HEY, TRY THESE

Portuguese sweet bread French toast with Nutella and raspberry sauce, curried tofu scramble, pressed sandwich with pesto and grilled vegetables, red lentil soup, crab cakes with jicama slaw and chipotle aioli, cookie a la mode.

TASTING NOTES

BOSTON • CAMBRIDGE

**MELINDA JONES AND TOM CLACKETT** had a modest desire. Much as they love East Boston, where they have lived for more than a decade, they pined for a casual, inexpensive, walk-to neighborhood cafe. Eastie has no shortage of Italian restaurants and taquerias. But if you wanted a brunch spot — the type with espresso and a wireless connection — you were out of luck. "We kept thinking, 'That's exactly the kind of place East Boston needs. Somebody should do that,'" recalls Jones. "And somehow we decided that somebody should be us." ❖ Jones, a nurse practitioner, and Clackett, a contractor, bought a broken-down building in Jeffries Point and turned it into a beauty. The city cooperated. The neighborhood rallied around them. And customers are coming in droves. ❖ With its tin ceiling, exposed brick walls, and chalkboard menu, the cafe is hip. The hordes of 30-somethings who flock here daily are obviously euphoric the place exists. The food can be wonderful. But there's a catch. As a neighborhood gathering spot, 303 Cafe is a fabulous success. As a restaurant, its ambitions sometimes outpace its abilities. ❖ What was intended to be a simple breakfast-and-lunch spot when it opened has rapidly morphed into a full-service operation. It now offers beer and wine, free delivery, a half-dozen homemade desserts, and entrees like pan-seared tilapia with mango salsa and apricot couscous. So much for coffee and eggs! ❖ The simple foods are where the 303 Cafe excels. Chunky red lentil soup ($4-$6), lightly seasoned with curry, is outstanding. "Melinda's salad" ($6.50-$7) is a creative blend of romaine, chick peas, sunflower seeds, red onion, carrots, and feta presented with artistic flair: a sliver of cucumber encircles the mixture like an edible wall. ❖ I'd go back any time for the grilled veggie sandwich ($7.50) of zucchini, summer squash, button mushrooms, plum tomatoes, and pesto on crusty sourdough. And seafood is consistently top-notch, including chunky crab cakes ($9.50) with crunchy jicama slaw and chipotle aioli. ❖ For breakfast, curried tofu scramble ($6) tossed with onions, mushrooms, and chick peas is delicious, and Portuguese sweet bread French toast ($7) layered with Nutella and raspberry sauce is ethereal. For dessert, a fat cookie (chocolate chunk, peanut butter, or oatmeal-raisin) with vanilla ice cream ($2.50) is perfection. But what should be a hot, gooey center in the "death by chocolate" molten cake ($6.25) is baked solid. ❖ Good news: This spot is such a welcome and obviously beloved addition to the neighborhood that we're willing to forgive its faults. Besides, we can't help but admire a place whose reach sometimes exceeds its grasp.

SACHA PFEIFFER, *Globe Staff*

# Gitlo's Dim Sum Bakery

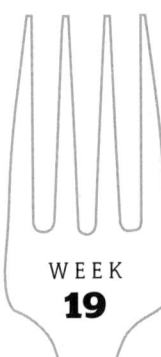

WEEK **19**

*164 Brighton Ave., Allston*
*617-782-2253*
*MasterCard and Visa accepted.*
*Wheelchair accessible; bathroom is accessible but next door.*
**PRICES** *$2.65-$4.75.*
**HOURS** *11 a.m.-10:30 p.m., daily.*
**ALCOHOL** *None.*

### HEY, TRY THESE

Shrimp dumplings, scallop shumai, Cantonese dumplings, XO sauce daikon cake, pan-fried daikon cake, sweet potato puff, char siu bao, rainbow clear noodles, seafood rice in lotus leaf, custard cream bun.

TASTING NOTES

**HE CALLS HIMSELF THE "DIM SUM SNOB."** When Richard Li of Somerville wrote to suggest we review "a new OUTSTANDING dim sum place in Allston," he made his case for Gitlo's Dim Sum Bakery this way: ❖ I "have not eaten dim sum in Boston in years except under intense peer pressure, but I've been to Gitlo's six times this year already (they opened in December). Well worth a trip." ❖ Li, a 29-year-old marketing director for Red Hat software company, is the toughest kind of dim sum critic for two reasons. First, he compares most dim sum treats — from fresh rice noodles to pork-filled steamed buns — with the Cantonese-style cooking of his mother. Second, he fell in love with dim sum in Hong Kong, the standard-bearer for this brunch-time meal, and it ruined him. ❖ Gitlo's is the reverse of the Chinatown dim sum scene. No carts. No chaos. No limited hours (Gitlo's serves dim sum all day, every day). Just a no-frills menu and a wunderkind chef, 24-year-old Deng Laing of Hong Kong, in a quiet, spare storefront with just 20 seats. ❖ We started with shrimp dumplings ($3.25) gorgeous enough to display in a curio cabinet. They are pudgy with a delicate filling of juicy shrimp, capped with a dollop of flying fish roe, and draped in expertly thin, pearly white wrappers. ❖ Steamed scallop shumai ($3.50) tucked mouth-watering shrimp, scallop, and pork into tender wonton wrappers. Pan-fried Cantonese dumplings ($3.25) burst with the plucky flavors of chives, crunchy watercress, and fresh ginger. ❖ Happily, the word "homemade" dominates the menu. The dumplings, puff pastry (try the sweet potato puffs, $2.95), and daikon cakes (don't miss the spicy XO sauce daikon cake, $2.95) are from scratch, as are the fluffy, white, half-moon-shaped filled buns (try the char siu bao with barbecued pork, $3.50, or the cream buns oozing with warm, sweet custard, $2.65). Most impressive, though, are the clear rice noodles rolled out daily. Stir-fried with ham, veggies, and mushrooms ($3.75), they offer just the right elasticity and chew. ❖ But all this home cooking can have its downside. Dishes sometimes run out. Others are slow to arrive. "It's always fresh. That's why we run out," explained owner Shi "Gitlo" Liu. ❖ A former Boston cabbie, Liu opened Gitlo's partly because he found weekend dim sum hours inconvenient. But mostly he felt his cousin Laing, who spent the last eight years honing his skills in a Hong Kong dim sum kitchen, needed an audience here. It was a good move. One that requires no peer pressure to support.

DENISE TAYLOR, *Globe Correspondent*

# Chipotle Mexican Grill

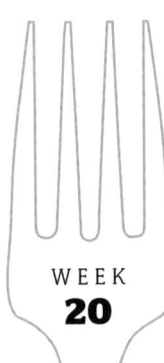

WEEK **20**

*1924 Beacon St. (Cleveland Circle), Brighton, 617-232-0788; 270-276 Elm St. (Davis Square), Somerville, 617-623-1759; 616 Fellsway, Medford, 781-393-6871*

*www.chipotle.com*

*All major credit cards accepted.*

**PRICES** *75 cents to $6.75.*

**HOURS** *Daily 11 a.m.-10 p.m.*

**ALCOHOL** *Beer at Medford, Dedham and Framingham locations (see review).*

### HEY, TRY THESE

Carnitas or barbacoa burrito, chicken salad, tomatillo-red chili, chips and guacamole.

TASTING NOTES
_____
_____
_____
_____

B O S T O N  •  C A M B R I D G E

**MY FRIENDS WILL TELL YOU** I wouldn't be caught dead in a fast-food place, though the truth of the matter is, when I had a thing for McDonald's fries, I went all the time. All that has changed, and now my friends are right. ❖ The folks at Chipotle Mexican Grill are quick to tell you that theirs isn't fast food, but rather "quick service." This growing chain delivers sanitized burrito places, with nearly identical layouts, galvanized tin walls, stainless-steel tabletops, and a green outlook. ❖ There's a certain arrogance to where they open — very close to similar but smaller burrito chains. Chipotle was started in Colorado in 1993 by Steve Ells, a graduate of the Culinary Institute of America and former cook at Stars in San Francisco. There are more than 700 locations, all company-owned. McDonald's was an investor for seven years, which allowed Chipotle to expand. According to spokeswoman Katherine Newell Smith, McDonald's "completely divested in 2006." ❖ I ate at three locations — in Cleveland Circle in Brighton, Davis Square in Somerville, and Medford (there are others in Dedham, Peabody, North Quincy, Braintree, Harvard Square, and Framingham). This food is indeed fresh, it's made quickly, it mostly tastes very good, and the quality is evident. Counter workers are gracious, and the eateries are spotless. ❖ You can order a burrito, which begins with a warm flour tortilla that's heaped with grilled chicken, steak, carnitas (braised pork), or barbacoa (spicy shredded beef), and black or pinto beans, along with cilantro-lime rice, plus add-ons: cheese, sour cream, salsa ($5.60-$6.45). Any of these come without the tortilla or as a salad (try grilled chicken, black beans, and hot salsa). On one visit, the chicken was hard and dry, the steak was tough on another, but all the beans were juicy and almost meaty, carnitas and barbacoa were both impressively spicy. Long-cooked meats and beans are made in Chicago and shipped out. ❖ Other choices are tacos, three crisp corn tortillas or soft wheat tortillas with burrito fillings, or house-made chips (75 cents), which were thick and just OK once and very crisp the other times, with several dipping sauces ($1.50 with chips); tomatillo-red chili, the hottest, is the best. Bright green guacamole is too smooth but delightful anyway. ❖ Chipotle delivers quality and service. The irony is that they're doing a good job being the anti-McDonald's.

SHERYL JULIAN, *Globe Staff*

**SOMERVILLE • BEYOND**

# The Fat Cat

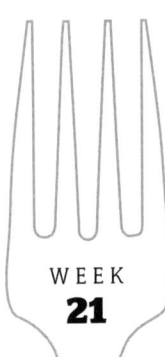

WEEK **21**

*24 Chestnut St., Quincy*
*617-471-4363*
*www.fatcatrestaurant.com*
*All major credit cards accepted.*
*Wheelchair accessible.*
**PRICES** *$4-$24.*
**HOURS** *Daily. 11 a.m.-1 a.m.*
**ALCOHOL** *Full liquor license.*

### HEY, TRY THESE

Barbecue pork nachos, garlic and parsley fries, Fat Cat wings, lobster mac 'n' cheese, Fat Cat burger, baked haddock, baby-back ribs, thick-as-a-brick brownie sundae.

**TASTING NOTES**
___
___
___
___
___

BOSTON • CAMBRIDGE

**THE FAT CAT IS A THROW-BACK** to pre-health food days: There are lots of sauces and creams on the menu. "It's not called 'The Skinny Cat,'" owner Neil Kiley notes wryly.

❖ Whatever, it makes for a good neighborhood gastropub where the fries come with dipping sauces, the burgers are gargantuan, and the mac 'n' cheese is loaded with lobster. Elastic-waist pants are your best bet here. ❖ Kiley was born and raised in Quincy, where he still lives with his wife, Nicole, who helps manage the place. The chef is Tom Coleman, late of Fifty Three South in Norwell. ❖ The 65-seat restaurant, in a historic building, has exposed brick walls and an industrial ceiling. A glass partition divides the long bar from the dining area; there are the usual flat-screen TVs — and a big sketch of a fat cat looking over the kitchen window. ❖ Though the lobster mac 'n' cheese ($16 and enough for two) is the biggest seller, Kiley says he loves the loaded fat dog ($6), a "gourmet hot dog" with a choice of several toppings. ❖ Try the fried dill pickle slices ($6), lightly battered and served with Cajun remoulade. Then it's on to hot and crisp hand-cut fries ($7), which arrive in a conical basket. You choose the spice and sauce. We opt for garlic and parsley with blue cheese, delicious and piquant. ❖ Fat Cat wings come the same way (10 wings for $7, 25 for $16, 50 for $30): pick mild, medium, or "XXX" heat and choose one of eight sauces. The wings are moist and spicy, with a nice kick. ❖ The Fat Cat takes American food and adds a twist. Consider the barbecue pork nachos ($8), a platter with surprisingly sweet and smoky chopped barbecue and caramelized onions, roasted garlic, and gooey manchego and cheddar. Decadent lobster mac 'n' cheese, the signature dish, contains generous lobster in a four-cheese sauce over corkscrew pasta with a scattering of panko crumbs and small grilled tomatoes. ❖ Grilled burgers ($7) are 10 ounces, stuffed into a thick ciabatta roll, and served with homemade fries. Toppings include avocado, fried onion rings, and cheeses (50 cents each). Tasty, but I'd go for a lighter roll. ❖ You won't have room for dessert (all $6), but don't let that stop you. There's a baker on the premises. The warm and fudgy thick-as-a-brick brownie sundae comes with vanilla ice cream, and butterscotch, raspberry, and chocolate drizzles. ❖ A wine and beer list is respectable, but best are cat-theme cocktails ($8 each), such as Alley Cat and The Fuzzy Kitten. Meow.

BELLA ENGLISH, *Globe Staff*

# Snappy Sushi

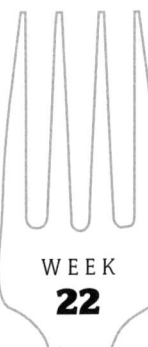

**WEEK 22**

420 Highland, Davis Square, Somerville
617-625-0400
www.snappysushi.com
All major credit cards accepted.
Wheelchair accessible.

**PRICES** Appetizers and salads: $3-$10. "Donburi" rice bowl dinners: $10-$16. Maki rolls: $3-$14. Nigiri: $1-$2 per piece.

**HOURS** Mon-Thu 11:30 a.m.-10 p.m., Fri-Sat 11:30 a.m.-11 p.m., Sun 11:30 a.m.-10 p.m.

**ALCOHOL** None.

### HEY, TRY THESE

Ika Sansai smoked squid, tuna tataki salad, "tuna gone wild" roll, Newbury fashion roll, mamemaki roll, Snappy's Triple Lunch box, miso soup, any nigiri.

TASTING NOTES
_____
_____
_____
_____
_____

BOSTON • CAMBRIDGE

**SNAPPY SUSHI IS NOT OPERATING** in your comfort zone. Their rice is a daring brown, seating is communal, and "fancy rolls" are boundary pushers that borrow from other cuisines. In short, this Davis Square newcomer is gleefully breaking all the rules. ❖ Step into the clean-lined modern space with its pale green-tea-colored walls and you can't miss owner Kazu Aotani's first bold move. Other than four sushi bar seats, Snappy has just one giant communal table that seats 12. It's a glossy pine beauty left behind by the previous longtime occupant, La Contessa Bakery, which used it for rolling out dough. ❖ More daring is Snappy's choice to offer brown rice only. It's brown koshihikari rice, which they mill in-house and use both at Snappy and at its sister restaurant, Shino Express Sushi on Newbury Street in Back Bay. Koshihikari, Japan's most revered white rice, is brown in its whole-grain form, before milling. ❖ Nigiri, sliced fish on fingers of seasoned rice, is cheap here at $1 per piece for most items. More intensely flavored fish such as mackerel ($1) and eel ($1) hold up well with the rice, as does creamy sea urchin ($2). Subtler selections like striped bass ($1) or halibut ($1) enter the realm of debate. The strong taste of the rice detracts from the delicate fish, but for those seeking a healthier meal, that may be a fair trade. In the fancy rolls with numerous ingredients, the subtly nutty taste of the rice mostly adds to the mix of flavors. ❖ Our complaints are with the inconsistency of the items. Some rolls are tight and some fish cut correctly. Others are not. On one visit the rice is gently seasoned, the next it is too sweet. One time the fish is fresh and buttery soft, another it is icy in the center. ❖ Otherwise, lunch specials are a bargain, salad greens fresh, and appetizers interesting and gorgeously plated. ❖ Fans of outrageous rolls will also find much to try here. Tufts of microgreens, swirling drizzles, and unusual maki roll wrappers such as bean, soy, and vegetable sheets keep things interesting. From the "tuna gone wild" roll ($7.95) capped with torched white tuna and citrusy yuzu sauce to the mamemaki tuna-avocado roll ($8.95), wrapped in a nicely chewy bean sheet and squirted with edamame (soybean) sauce, the fancy rolls get positively rococo. ❖ As for the unusual flourishes like pineapple salsa, pesto, and roasted garlic sauce, some are inspired; others taste fine but feel out of place. ❖ Still, it's hard not to admire an irreverent menu and concept that leads rather than follows.

DENISE TAYLOR, *Globe Correspondent*

# Emma's

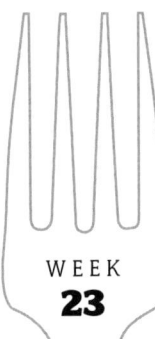

WEEK **23**

40 Hampshire St., Cambridge (Kendall Square)
617-864-8534
www.emmaspizza.com
All major credit cards accepted.
Wheelchair accessible (restaurant has a ramp that can be put down as needed).

**PRICES** $4.95-$15 (some large pizzas range higher).

**HOURS** Mon-Fri 11:30 a.m.-10 p.m., Sat 4-10 p.m.

**ALCOHOL** Beer and wine.

### HEY, TRY THESE

Marinated goat cheese, salad of greens, spinach salad, grilled chicken sandwich, pizza with traditional sauce and cheese (and all variations).

**TASTING NOTES**
_____
_____
_____
_____

BOSTON • CAMBRIDGE

**EMMA'S PIZZA** on Cambridge's Huron Avenue had a cult following even though Emma was so grumpy most of the time she wouldn't look up when you ordered your pie. Cranky Emma Matschichelian and her obliging husband, Gregory, hung up their aprons after 29 years of making pizzas for the Brattle Street crowd. ❖ Wendy Saver and David Rockwood bought the business in 1995; they had a lease and paid rent to the Matschichelians, who still owned the building. Emma's old clientele was happy to find very enthusiastic pizza makers in the old space. ❖ What the neighbors also found was a beautiful thin-crusted pizza, with fine salads and homemade dressing. You could ask for sausage and pepperoni, but you could also get roasted peppers and broccoli. ❖ Things went well until Emma died a few years ago and Gregory refused to offer the couple anything more definitive than a month-by-month lease. So they took their business elsewhere — to a 40-seat place on Hampshire Street, where the space is roomy enough so the wait isn't as endless as it was in the old days. ❖ Thin-crusted pizzas pop out of the oven, and the menu includes marinated goat cheese, good salads, pressed sandwiches, and a cheap but stylish wine list. You can't beat simplicity for a winning formula. ❖ I like traditional tomato sauce, mozzarella, and a crisp, thin crust ($9 for a 12-inch pie; $12 for 16-inches). That's what Emma's does best. The toppings make up a long list and include dried cranberries, roasted mushrooms, roasted gold potatoes, hot cherry peppers, broccoli, and caramelized onions (add $1.25 or $1.75 per topping or order one of Emma's "Pizza Suggestions," $11.50-$21). You can have goat cheese or sheep cheese or no cheese at all. The other sauces include a spicier tomato sauce with rosemary and a simple olive oil infused with garlic. ❖ Emma's pressed sandwiches are quite fabulous. Made on focaccia in an electric press, one is filled with gorgeous grilled chicken breast, house-roasted tomato, grilled onions, house-smoked bacon, and smoked mozzarella ($7.95). Another contains grilled yellow squash, roasted red peppers, fresh sliced tomato, red onion, goat cheese, and cilantro ($7.25). ❖ The salads are voluptuous — greens with homemade croutons and red-wine vinaigrette or roasted-garlic balsamic dressing ($5.95), and baby spinach with marinated artichokes and a Pommery mustard dressing ($6.50; $7.25 with Feta cheese). There's also a nice little goat cheese appetizer marinated in fresh herbs served on a bed of greens. ❖ Most of Emma's regulars from the old neighborhood kept their promise of visiting them in Kendall Square. And Saver and Rockwood still make them happy.

SHERYL JULIAN, *Globe Staff*

SOMERVILLE • BEYOND

# Flour Bakery + Cafe

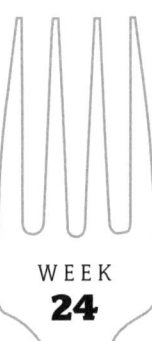

WEEK **24**

*1595 Washington St., Boston (South End)*
*617-267-4300*
*www.flourbakery.com*
*All major credit cards accepted.*
*Fully accessible.*
**PRICES** *$1.25 -$10.95.*
**HOURS** *Mon-Fri 7 a.m.-9 p.m., Sat 8 a.m.-6 p.m., Sun 9 a.m.-3 p.m. (Sun 9 a.m.-5 p.m. May-Oct.)*
**ALCOHOL** *None.*

### HEY, TRY THESE

Sour cream coffee cake, brioche au sucre, pound cake, lemon curd and raspberry jam cake, roast chicken sandwich, roast beef sandwich, quiche, gazpacho, peanut butter cookie, chocolate cookies.

**TASTING NOTES**

---

**BOSTON · CAMBRIDGE**

**WHEN JOANNE CHANG** opened Flour Bakery + Cafe several years ago on the first floor of a new building that houses the South End Community Health Center, 39 condominiums, and a new Walgreen's, she and her staff were getting worried about her decision to stay open until 7 p.m. Breakfast and lunch were both doing fine, but afternoons were deadly. Once an hour, she says, a customer would trickle in for a cup of coffee.

❖ "Now," says Chang, "it's constant." People stream in for snacks, supper to go, and pastries and celebration cakes to take to dinner parties. ❖ Success couldn't have happened to a nicer person. Chang offers a smile all the time, she works very long hours, and she's immensely talented. Her tables are filled with some of Boston's hippest customers, and other restaurateurs frequent Flour in their off hours. ❖ The bakery goods are a lively mix of simple American confections and complicated French pastries. Sitting beside an incredible sour cream coffee cake, for instance (breakfast cakes like these vary from $2.25 for a scone to $2.75 for a huge slice of this light luscious cake), is a homemade croissant, a square of apple-snacking spice cake, a sticky pecan bun, a tender brioche, and soft, roasted peanuty cookies. ❖ Chang's lemon curd tarts (individual tarts are $4.95) are treasures of flaky dough and deep lemon-butter richness, her Scharffen Berger double chocolate cookies are intense and dreamy. ❖ Chang's bakers make their own breads for sandwiches ($7.50), which change all the time. The bread is tender with a beautiful, fine crumb. The roast chicken sandwich is packed with reddish achiote- and tomato-marinated chicken with strips of jicama, and guacamole made with avocado, chipotle, cilantro, and limes. As if the meat were not creamy enough, the avocado spread adds a spoonful of piquant richness. ❖ All the sandwich fillings can be ordered as salads, which are tender, young greens. Soups change daily. The quiches ($5.50) have creamy custards, baked so the eggs aren't watery in their flaky crusts. Even the ice tea is real and homemade. ❖ There is a hangout quality to the place. Sunlight floods the room. A big communal table in the center is filled with newspapers and magazines, so you can find yourself sitting between a doctor in scrubs (Boston University Medical Center is just down the street), a construction worker, and a young man with shaved legs and manicured toenails. ❖ So Flour has everything: quality that's hard to find in a place with such a simple concept, and a little something to look at.

SHERYL JULIAN, *Globe Staff*

# Peppercornz on Main

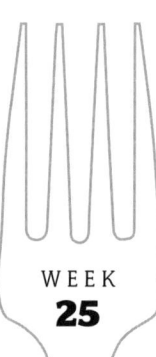

*1037 Main St., South Weymouth*
*781-331-9931*
*www.peppercornz.com*
*All major credit cards accepted.*
*Wheelchair accessible.*
**PRICES** *$2.99 to $17.*

WEEK **25**

**HOURS** *Tue-Thu 11 a.m.-9 p.m., Fri 11 a.m.-10 p.m., Sat 4 p.m.-10 p.m., Sun 9 a.m.-2 p.m. (brunch)*
**ALCOHOL** *Full liquor license.*

### HEY, TRY THESE

Artichoke bites, portobello mushroom salad, Sedona pizza, gnocchi, Lone Star burger, lemon icebox pie.

**TASTING NOTES**

BOSTON • CAMBRIDGE

**ONE OF THE OWNERS** of Peppercornz, Linda Varraso, comes from a large Italian family in the Boston area. Her imprint is on the handmade gnocchi and other pastas, meatballs, pizza, and calzone. The other owner, Taylor Beckett, is from California, hence the abundance of dishes with avocado and names like Catalina, Pasadena, and Laguna. ❖ It's a happy marriage of the two cultures, with dishes that are both creative and fresh. Beckett runs the marketing side; Varraso the kitchen. She and her five siblings grew up in Braintree with working parents who would take meat out of the freezer in the morning, leaving instructions for the children to make dinner that night. ❖ Their parents were always complimentary but added comments such as "maybe a little less salt next time" or "perhaps a little more garlic." And both grandmothers taught the kids how to roll pasta and make gnocchi on a huge wooden cutting board. Varraso went on to earn an MBA, for which she had to write a business plan for a restaurant. That became Peppercornz. But Varraso knew if she really wanted to open her own place, she needed professional training, so she took classes at the Baltimore International Culinary College. ❖ Start with artichoke bites ($6.99), soft orbs of chopped artichoke hearts and three cheeses breaded and deep-fried to golden, crispy perfection. Parmesan adds tang, mild cheddar and mozzarella the nice gooey texture. For more kick, drag them through the accompanying cream cheese and salsa dip. ❖ Not to be missed is gnocchi ($11.99), which Varasso has been making since she was "in single digits." But she substitutes ricotta for the usual potato, and it shows in the pasta's lightness. ("My father called my grandmother's gnocchi 'lead sinkers,'" says Varraso.) We tried it with a delicate tomato cream sauce; it also comes with marinara. And crunchy, garlicky toast. ❖ A friend whose women's group goes to Peppercornz regularly recommended two pizzas: ranchero ($12.49) or Sedona ($10.99). Sedona is loaded with artichokes, sun-dried tomatoes, chopped garlic, goat cheese, and caramelized onions, with only olive oil. Without a red or white sauce, the homemade crust shines. No matter how stuffed you are, try the lemon icebox pie ($3.59). It's incredibly light and very lemony. Next time, though, we'll save room for individual chocolate or apple pie pizza ($5.59). ❖ Varraso's parents, Al and Carmela, are still their daughter's head culinary fans. Al delivers orders for Peppercornz two days a week at lunch, while Carmela handles the bookkeeping. "Proud doesn't begin to describe it," says Varraso.

BELLA ENGLISH, *Globe Staff*

# Dok Bua Thai Kitchen

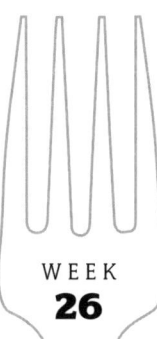

*411 Harvard St., Brookline*
*617-232-2955*
*www.dokbuathai.com*
*All major credit cards accepted. Fully accessible.*
**PRICES** *$3.95-$15.95.*
**HOURS** *Mon-Sat 11 a.m.-10:30 p.m., Sun 11 a.m.-10 p.m.*
**ALCOHOL** *None.*

WEEK **26**

## HEY, TRY THESE

Chicken satay, larb (ground chicken salad), som tum (papaya salad), pad si ew (rice noodles with chicken), kai jeaw koong sub (Thai omelet), pla neung manao (steamed fish with lemon sauce), pad ma kue yao (eggplant with chili), poo-nim (crispy soft-shell crab).

TASTING NOTES

BOSTON • CAMBRIDGE

**DOK BUA IS OWNED** by Thailand-born Nida Pong and has been in this spot near the Allston Village edge of Brookline for the better part of a decade. About four years ago, it expanded its restaurant tables to seat approximately 30. Then, friends started mentioning the restaurant to me as a place they'd recently discovered. What began as a market and restaurant — located between Wulf's, the famous Brookline fish market, and the bagel emporium Kupel's — has over the years morphed into an eatery where the friendliest service meets some pretty terrific Thai food ❖ This spot does two of my favorite dishes quite well. One is pad si ew ($9.95), a variation of pad Thai. Si ew doesn't fuss with all the chopped egg bits and bean sprouts common to pad Thai. Instead, it consists of very wide rice noodles cooked with pieces of chicken and Chinese broccoli. The dark sauce barely coats the noodles, so the dish tastes light, the vegetable crisp, and the morsels of chicken caramel-like. ❖ Som tum ($7.95) is the other dish I look for. Made from very thin and long matchsticks of green papaya, which are white and quite crisp, and tossed with a hot vinegary dressing, the salad also contains green beans, tomatoes, and peanuts. You can imagine eating this salad in tropical weather and feeling incredibly refreshed. ❖ The best item on the menu is poo-nim ($15.95), which is billed as "crispy soft-shell crab." What arrives is a mountain of claws from cut-up soft shells that are dipped in a tempura-like batter and fried until golden brown. ❖ Pla neung manao ($15.95) consists of a foot-long steamed bass bathed in a lemony broth. Cooked with its head and bones intact, the flaky meat tastes especially sweet. A salad called larb ($8.95), a kind of spicy chili mixture, is offered with chicken or meat. It's finely chopped, cooked, and mixed with a limey dressing, mint leaves, red onion, and cucumber, presented on a bed of lettuce. Also delightfully hot is pla goong ($9.95), a grilled shrimp salad with celery, quartered button mushrooms, and lemon grass on a bed of greens. ❖ If you don't like heat, better say so early on. As for takeout, Dok Bua packs its dishes so they don't leak all over your car on the way home. The containers have a nice, tight seal. But this food, with its crunchy and crisp textures, isn't as good at home. Greens wilt, deep-fried items get soggy, and the crunch is lost. So settle in and enjoy these exceptional dishes as they emerge from the pan.

SHERYL JULIAN, *Globe Staff*

# Ball Square
## Cafe & Breakfast

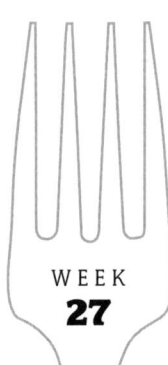

WEEK **27**

*708 Broadway, Somerville*
*617-623-2233*
*All major credit cards accepted. Wheelchair accessible.*
**PRICES** *Breakfast: $2-$9. Lunch: $4-$9.*
**HOURS** *Daily 6:30 a.m.-3 p.m.*
**ALCOHOL** *None.*

### HEY, TRY THESE

Black-bean salsa omelet, Belgian waffle, chocolate chip-coconut pancakes, Omar's home fries, grilled chicken avocado wrap, turkey club, sweet potato fries.

**TASTING NOTES**

**IT'S BEING CALLED THE BREAKFAST WAR.** ❖ On one side of the battlefield is Sound Bites, which earned perverse popularity for owner Yasser Mirza's tyrannical insistence that customers scram once they swallow their last bite of food. On the other side is Ball Square Cafe & Breakfast, a newcomer run by the affable Mike Moccia, who took over the Sound Bites space last summer when Mirza moved next door. ❖ Why the hostility? It stems from their disagreement over whether Mirza was kicked out of his old spot by his former landlord (Moccia's father, who owns Victor's Deli on the same block), or whether they simply couldn't agree on a new lease. ❖ The good news is food lovers now have two choices for high-quality eats, especially gut-busting breakfasts, in Ball Square. Their prices and kitchen offerings are virtual copycats. But Ball Square Cafe is the smaller, less-hectic of the two, and the place where (at least for now) you're not as likely to wait for a table. ❖ Moccia handsomely renovated the 40-seat restaurant. His co-owner is head cook Omar Djebbouri, who used to work at Sound Bites — another source of acrimony. ❖ It's hard to go wrong with Djebbouri's cooking. He makes gorgeous, fluffy omelets ($6.50 to $8.95) with inspired fillings, like smoked salmon and baby spinach, or black-bean salsa, or asparagus and prosciutto. Belgian waffles ($4.50 to $7.50) are so light they're like biting into air. And they're lovely heaped with whipped cream and fresh fruit. ❖ Pancakes ($3.95 to $6.95) are grilled to a tawny brown, then stuffed with fillings such as tart cranberries, fresh mango, and seasonal blackberries. My favorite: chocolate chip-coconut, a gooey-chewy combo that melds into a warm mess. ❖ The fruit bowl ($4.50) has a selection not often found at cheap eats joints - papaya, kiwi, pineapple, cantaloupe, honeydew, raspberries, and more. Cinnamony French toast ($2.50 to $6.95) is made with challah. For a decadent side order, try "Omar's home fries," a blend of mashed potatoes, sour cream, and garlic, all fried on the griddle. ❖ Although most of Moccia's business comes from breakfast, I had a pleasing lunch here, too. Grilled chicken avocado wrap ($7.50) is a standout, with its warm meat and perfectly ripe avocado. Sweet potato fries need salt, but they're hand-cut into fat wedges and aren't the least bit greasy. ❖ During cold weather, customers are hit with an icy blast each time the front door opens. So until spring arrives, bundle up if you visit — because that frigid draft is almost as frosty as the chill coming from the neighbor next door.

SACHA PFEIFFER, *Globe Staff*

# El Oriental de Cuba

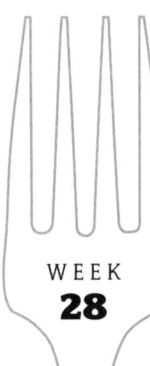

**WEEK 28**

*416 Centre St., Jamaica Plain*
*617-524-6464*
*www.elorientaldecuba.com*
*All major credit cards accepted.*
*Wheelchair accessible.*

**PRICES** *Breakfast: $3.75-$5.50. Lunch and dinner: $1.75-$22.95 (only three items over $15).*
**HOURS** *Mon-Thu 8 a.m.-9 p.m., Fri-Sat 8 a.m.-10 p.m., Sun 8 a.m.-8 p.m.*
**ALCOHOL** *None.*

### HEY, TRY THESE

Stuffed potatoes, fried yucca, black beans, ropa vieja, rice with octopus, seafood stew, flan.

**TASTING NOTES**
_____
_____
_____
_____
_____

**BOSTON • CAMBRIDGE**

**IN MIAMI, THERE'S A PLACE** like El Oriental de Cuba on practically every corner and in every strip mall — a spot where neighborhood residents, beat cops, businessmen, and the occasional gringo tourists come for authentic Cuban specialties and tropical fruit drinks. ❖ If you're looking for a Cuban fix, you'll probably head to Jamaica Plain's El Oriental, a JP institution since the early '90s. A fire closed it in July 2005 (arson was suspected) and the restaurant reopened after major renovations and help from the neighborhood and city in October 2006. ❖ At dinner, one of our group, a native of Cuba, orders ropa vieja ($11.95), a large bowl of shredded beef in a rich broth with onions and red and green peppers. He announces that the dish tastes much like what he ate in Havana, except this one has more vegetables. A chicken version ($11.95) is equally savory. ❖ Rice with octopus ($13.95) is a huge plate groaning with rice made slightly spicy with red pepper and liberally dotted with chunks of tender meat. Cuban food isn't usually hot, so this dish is a surprise. Owner Nobel ("Like the prize") Garcia, who is Cuban, says that while he offers many traditional dishes, the menu has been influenced by customers from Central and South America and other parts of the Caribbean. ❖ For example, seafood stew with rice ($16.95), is flavored with fish stock and plenty of shrimp, octopus bits, and mussels. Cilantro garnishes the broth. Sirloin butt steak ($12.95) is a disappointingly bland, pallid piece of meat. A mound of caramelized onions covering the steak turns out to be the best part. ❖ Main dishes come with rice, black beans, which have a wonderful earthy flavor; maduros, tostones, or French fries. Tostones (twice-fried green plaintains) are crisp on the outside, tender inside, but lack salt. Maduros (fried sweet plaintains), a particular favorite from my childhood in Miami, are not nearly sweet or soft enough on our first visit. Another time, maduros are sweet and tender, almost perfect. ❖ Milkshakes with mango, guava, guanabana, mamey, and tamarind ($3 each) are so thick and rich, they could double as dessert. ❖ Desserts are made on the premises, and include a version of dulce de leche ($2), rice pudding ($2), guava shells filled with cream cheese ($2.95), and flan ($2). Flan is the winner, with a wonderful eggy, vanilla flavor and a beautiful caramelized sugar sauce. ❖ There may be times in winter when you'll hop a plane to South Florida. But if you can't, warm your body and spirit at El Oriental de Cuba.

ANN LUISA, CORTISSOZ, *Globe Staff*

# Pie Bakery & Cafe

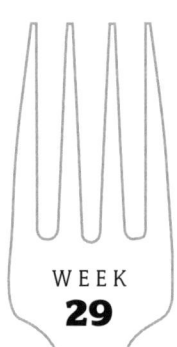

*796 Beacon St., Newton Center*

*617-332-8743*

*All major credit cards accepted. Wheelchair accessible.*

**PRICES** *Breakfast: $1-$4.95. Lunch: $4.95-$7.95. Dinner: $5.50-$15.95.*

**HOURS** *Mon-Fri 7 a.m.-8 p.m., Sat 8 a.m.-8 p.m., Sun 8 a.m.- 6 p.m.*

**ALCOHOL** *None.*

WEEK **29**

### HEY, TRY THESE

Egg pie by the slice, chicken and apple compote pasty, spinach and feta pie, potato knish, onion soup, beef chili, key lime pie.

TASTING NOTES
___
___
___
___
___

BOSTON • CAMBRIDGE

**YOU HAVE PROBABLY NEVER TASTED** an egg pie as ethereal as the one pastry chef Paige Retus is making at Pie Bakery & Cafe in Newton Center. This handsome slice has the look of quiche, and it's made from a similar eggy base, but Retus has managed to produce a custard so rich and so smooth and a pastry so flaky, you have to wonder if the filling wasn't cooked separately in a water bath, then carefully slipped into a rich pie crust. In fact, says Retus, a combination of sour cream, milk, and eggs, baked "long and low" gives these results. ❖ Egg pie ($5.50) might be flavored with spinach and mushrooms one day, ham the next, and it's just one of the outstanding pastries Retus is making for the food case. Her pasty of roast chicken with a little apple compote tucked into one end ($5.95) would make a Cornish miner's wife proud. (Pasty is pronounced with the same "a" as past, not paste.) ❖ With its storefront windows, butter cream-colored walls, bright lighting, and white sails covering industrial elements on the ceiling, Pie Bakery is a most cheerful place. Retus made her name in Todd English's kitchen at Olives. After that came blu, The Metropolitan Club, several consulting jobs in pastry kitchens around town, and then what she calls a "work-study" job at Flour Bakery + Cafe. ❖ Meanwhile, she was talking to Kaplansky about the pie venture. A graduate of the Cambridge School of Culinary Arts, Kaplansky was running Elli's Downstairs Cafe in East Cambridge. Ryan Costigan, also a Cambridge School graduate, makes the savory elements on the menu. ❖ At the counter, Kaplansky is a whirlwind. If you sit down at one of the 24 seats or stools along a marble counter overlooking the kitchen, she'll ladle hearty onion soup ($4.95) into a deep white pottery bowl. It's topped with a square of melted cheese on focaccia. ❖ No one overdoes sugar or salt here. A potato knish the size of a small melon ($4.95) is a delightful carb fest of spud plus pastry (and enough knish for four), but the potato-onion mixture is desperate for salt. Same with shepherd's pie ($6.95), the meaty filling cleverly topped with sweet potato puree but too bland below. A roast chicken dinner ($15.95) consists of a flavorful half-bird, skin crisp but meat a little dry, accompanied by a generous salad with balsamic dressing and an outstanding flaky spinach and feta pie. ❖ In a world where so many people shun carbs, the Retus-Kaplansky team has managed to draw crowds.

SHERYL JULIAN, *Globe Staff*

# Cambridge, 1

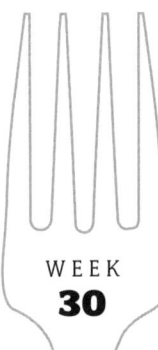

**WEEK 30**

*27 Church St. Cambridge (Harvard Square)*
*617-576-1111*
*www.cambridge1.us*
*All major credit cards accepted. Fully accessible.*
**PRICES** *$5-$24 (majority of items under $15).*
**HOURS** *Sun-Thu 11:30 a.m.-midnight, Fri-Sat 11:30 a.m.-1 a.m.*
**ALCOHOL** *Beer and wine.*

### HEY, TRY THESE

Bibb lettuce salad, grilled chicken and romaine salad, baby arugula salad, roasted onion and tomato pizza, Italian sausage pizza, potato and fontina pizza, tiramisu ice cream.

TASTING NOTES
_____
_____
_____
_____

BOSTON • CAMBRIDGE

**IT'S EXCITING TO FIND PEOPLE** who know what they're doing and make it a pleasure for the diner. The staff at Cambridge, 1 is awfully good at what they do, whether it's standing tableside to open a bottle of wine or serving you a pizza that will knock you out. ❖ Owners Chris Lutes and Matthew Curtis understand good food, know when to stop conceptualizing and get on with training staff, and have great taste. Cambridge, 1 looks industrial and sleek. It's friendly, with a lot of noise and a very limited menu — 13 pizzas, five salads, and a lone ice cream dessert — you either like it at once or you know it's not for you. From the crowd, it looks like pretty much everyone in shouting distance thinks it's for them. ❖ The restaurant seats 90, but some of those seats are at community tables and the management feels obliged to leave a little space between the parties, so there are fewer seats than it seems. The front of the house is mobbed with people waiting to get in, but in back, it's quiet. ❖ The pizzas here are terrific, made with a very thin dough, rolled into rough-shaped ovals and grilled over hardwood charcoal. You can buy a whole or a half and with either, you get a large serrated knife to cut them up. ❖ To make grilled pizzas, the dough is set over hot hardwood charcoals and cooked on one side. Then it's flipped over and a smattering of ingredients — red potatoes cut so thinly you can practically see through them ($8 for half, $15 for full); Italian sausage out of its case and crumbled all over the dough ($9 for half, $17 for full); small clusters of melted onions ($8 for half, $15 for full) — are sprinkled on the grilled side along with some cheese and seasonings. What emerges is something that tastes like crisp, hot crackers, with one or two intense flavors. The potatoes, for instance, are seasoned with garlic and rosemary, with real Parmesan and Romano scattered on the dough, little mounds of mashed potatoes piped here and there, and a few scallion brushes as garnish. ❖ The salads are beautiful and well dressed. Iceberg lettuce wedge ($6) has a creamy intense shallot dressing. Bibb leaves are lush with blue cheese and a Dijon vinaigrette ($8). A grilled chicken and romaine salad ($9) might be a meal. ❖ Even a contrived tiramisu ice cream ($5), which sounds insipid, is perfectly dreamy, a mixture of cake, chocolate, and cream presented in Toscanini's paper cups. Cambridge, 1 seems to have everything.

SHERYL JULIAN, *Globe Staff*

# Bangkok Cafe

WEEK **31**

25 Poplar St., Roslindale
617-327-8810
www.bangkok-cafe.com
All major credit cards accepted.
Wheelchair accessible.
**PRICES** $3.50-$14.95.
**HOURS** Tue-Thu and Sun 11:30 a.m.-9 p.m., Fri-Sat 11:30 a.m.-10 p.m. Closed Mon.
**ALCOHOL** Beer and wine.

### HEY, TRY THESE

Cafe sampler for two, crispy pad Thai, duck choo chee, crispy chicken Bangkok basil, Thai coconut custard, fried bananas.

TASTING NOTES
_____
_____
_____
_____
_____

**BOSTON • CAMBRIDGE**

**DANNY TITISUTTIKUL LEARNED TO COOK** back home in Thailand from his mother who, he says, used only the best, freshest ingredients. When he was 12, his mother was killed in a bus accident. The boy took over the family cooking chores, and attended culinary school in Bangkok. In 1984, he moved to Boston, working in several Thai restaurants before opening his own — the Bangkok Cafe in Foxborough — in 1992. ❖ He now has a second Bangkok Cafe, in Roslindale, facing Adams Park. It's a cozy, quiet place with 36 seats — a pleasant place to have a terrific meal. Ask Princess Ploypailin of Thailand, who as an MIT student visited the restaurant four times. ❖ Start with the cafe sampler for two ($9.95), which will give you a taste of crispy Thai rolls; Paradise beef in a sweet marinade; and butterflied shrimp fried in wonton skins — with a fiery sweet sauce. ❖ The menu rates the dishes from one star — "spicy" — to four — "suicidal!" Thankfully, we stuck with the two-star "hot and spicy," including crispy chicken Bangkok basil ($11.95), which made us reach for our water glasses. The chicken is deep-fried and then stir-fried with vegetables in a hot chili basil sauce. It's deliciously different. ❖ Titisuttikul uses no MSG and cooks only with canola oil. Several dishes have met the "Boston Best Bites" standards under a program that encourages restaurants to add heart-healthy options. ❖ We couldn't leave a Thai restaurant without trying a curry dish. Duck choo chee ($14.95) combines chunks of tender, boneless roast duck with baby corn, carrots, zucchini, tomatoes, and peppers. Sweet pineapple chunks and coconut milk help cut the heat of the red curry. As one customer summed it up in the guest book: "This curry rocks!" ❖ Under "Creative Cuisine," you can design your own meal from chicken, beef, seafood, duck, or tofu; one of seven sauces; and various rices or noodles. We picked scallops with ginger scallion sauce ($12.95) and were rewarded with plump morsels of seafood and a load of fresh ginger cut into matchsticks for crunch and flavor. Each dish comes with a side of stir-fried vegetables. ❖ Except for the ice cream, desserts are homemade. We loved the silkiness of the Thai coconut custard ($3), served slightly warm, and also the chunks of deep-fried bananas in tortillas ($3.95) drizzled with honey. ❖ Titisuttikul is 50 but looks at least 10 years younger. Maybe it's because, between his two restaurants, he's constantly eating his own health-conscious food. His culinary Fountain of Youth is a good enough reason to return.

BELLA ENGLISH, *Globe Staff*

# Tashi Delek

WEEK **32**

236 Washington St., Brookline

617-232-4200

www.tashidelekboston.com

All major credit cards accepted. Entrance is two steps up, but bathroom is wheelchair-friendly.

**PRICES** *Appetizers: $4-$12. Entrees: $12-$17. Tibetan hot pots (take half-hour to prepare): $20-$25.*

**HOURS** *Mon-Sat 11:30 a.m.-2:30 p.m. and 5-10 p.m. Closed Sunday.*

**ALCOHOL** *Full license.*

### HEY, TRY THESE

Momos, oatmeal soup, curried lentil soup, lhasa shapta (beef in tomato-ginger sauce), chu bu kha tsa (shrimp with yellow and green squash in red curry sauce), tofu with mixed vegetables, sho go khatsa (curried boiled potatoes), deysee (sweetened rice).

TASTING NOTES

BOSTON • CAMBRIDGE

**IN TIBET, FOOD IS FUEL.** To stay warm in the high altitude, Tibetans have historically eaten energy-rich mutton, yak meat, dried beef, barley flour, high-fat yak milk, and tea blended with salted butter. Root vegetables like turnips and potatoes were staples, since few veggies or fruits grew on the arid plateaus. ❖ So are yak and buttered tea on the menu at Tashi Delek in Brookline Village? Yak, no. Buttered tea, yes — as well as soups, simple salads, noodle dishes, the famous Tibetan dumplings called momos, and entrees of beef, chicken, shrimp, or greens. ❖ At Tashi Delek (Tibetan for hello and good luck), the food is prepared by chef-owner Lobsang Thargay, who opened the restaurant with his wife, Phurbu. The couple came to Boston in the 1990s through a resettlement program for Tibetans living in India and Nepal. ❖ Their restaurant is pretty and peaceful. A back counter is decorated with the eight auspicious symbols of Buddhism. "We are doing our best to preserve our culture," said Phurbu, "and tell that world that Tibet is still a country and we are keeping it alive." ❖ Lobsang, who studied at the Cambridge School of Culinary Arts, is a talent in the kitchen. His warming soups ($4-$5) are perfect for cool weather: shen dal, a thin curried lentil; jhasha thang, a sweet corn soup flecked with whole kernels; and, best of all, drothuk, oatmeal porridge speckled with ground beef. ❖ I also love his momos (appetizer $6.50, entree $14-$17), fat dumplings stuffed with pureed broccoli, cauliflower, and shiitakes; spinach and ricotta sweetened with sugar; tofu; or ground beef. The pasta wrappers are overly thick, but the fillings are richly flavorful. ❖ In many of the poultry and shrimp dishes, the meat is battered and lightly fried, which makes the chicken in the jha-sha mango salsa ($15) off-puttingly bready, despite its pleasantly fruity sauce. So we asked for sauteed shrimp in chu bu kha tsa ($16), a mix of yellow and green squash with zippy red curry, and the end result was delicious. ❖ Even better is lhasa shapta ($15), lean slices of tender beef in a light tomato sauce with ginger and scallions. Tofu tsel ne zom ($14), a stir-fry of tofu and mixed vegetables in tomato-garlic sauce, is also excellent. ❖ As for that buttered tea, known as bhod jha ($2), it's an acquired taste I've yet to acquire. "It tastes like drinking melted butter," a friend said. I prefer a sweet ending such as deysee ($3.50), sugared basmati rice with raisins, almonds, and a dollop of yogurt for lively tang.

SACHA PFEIFFER, *Globe Correspondent*

# Alfresco

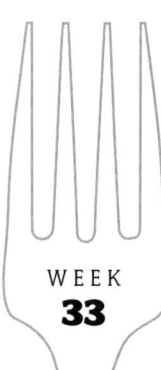

**WEEK 33**

382 Highland Ave., Davis Square, Somerville
617-776-8100
www.alfrescosomerville.com
MasterCard and Visa accepted.
Wheelchair accessible.
**PRICES** $3.95-$14.95.
**HOURS** 9 a.m.- 10 p.m. daily.
**ALCOHOL** Beer and wine.

### HEY, TRY THESE

Buttermilk pancakes, asparagus and tomato omelet, sauteed calamari, chicken carciofi.

**TASTING NOTES**

**BRUNCH HAS ALMOST BECOME A COMPETITIVE SPORT** around Boston, Cambridge, and Somerville. Alfresco, on the outskirts of Davis Square, is doing its part to meet the burgeoning brunch crowd's needs. ❖ Brunch at Alfresco on a Sunday afternoon (they serve until 3) is indeed a pleasant experience. The space is on the corner of Highland and Cutler avenues; there's not much in the way of decor, but it's a storefront space with big windows on two sides, and the tiny white lights strung above the windows give the room a festive feel. The brunch menu isn't extensive, but it has most of the requisite basics (besides waffles) in large quantities. ❖ Our very friendly server urges us to try the pancakes, so we get an order of buttermilk cakes ($3.25), which are golden and just a little crisp at the edges. They're light enough that you don't feel leaden after eating them, and the buttermilk provides a pleasant tang. ❖ The steak with two eggs ($9.95), served with home fries, toast, and seasonal fruit, is enough to keep a 12-year-old occupied for most of our meal. The omelets, served with the same accompaniments, have the perfect ratio of egg to filling. The asparagus and tomato ($8.99), full of asparagus tips and chunky bits of tomato, is savory and satisfying. The grilled salmon omelet ($9.99) doesn't incorporate the fish into the omelet, oddly; the salmon is served on the side, and it's overcooked. ❖ On an evening visit to sample Alfresco's Mediterranean-influenced dinner menu, however, the salmon special served with scallops over linguine in a pesto cream sauce is perfectly cooked (and is enough food for a couple of lunches as well). ❖ Owner Hussain Mohiddin says that his menu concentrates on Mediterranean flavors because part of his family is Italian and has owned restaurants in Italy. And Mohiddin certainly has a way with the Italian-style calamari (available at lunch and dinner, $7.95). The rings and tentacles are sautéed in olive oil and served with a chunky tomato and red pepper sauce that has us reaching for the bread to sop up every bit. ❖ The risotto with mushrooms ($10.95) is lighter and less earthy than we expected, with a lemon tang. The chicken carciofi ($14.95) make us sigh with pleasure, and a generous portion of roasted potatoes, zucchini, and carrots makes us sigh again. ❖ For now, it's easy to walk into Alfresco for brunch or dinner. But the food and the prices are so good that word is bound to get out.

ANN LUISA CORTISSOZ, *Globe Staff*

# Wonder Spice Cafe

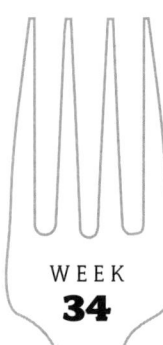

**WEEK 34**

*697 Centre St., Jamaica Plain*
*617-522-0200*
*All major credit cards accepted.*
*Wheelchair accessible.*
**PRICES** *$3-$15.95.*
**HOURS** *Sun-Thu 11:30 a.m.-10 p.m., Fri-Sat 11:30 a.m.-10:30 p.m.*
**ALCOHOL** *Beer and wine.*

### HEY, TRY THESE

Nem chhaw; any pad thai (crispy and southern are special); chili duck; emerald salmon; fried ice cream.

**TASTING NOTES**

---

**BOSTON • CAMBRIDGE**

**THE WONDER SPICE CAFE** is a family affair. It's owned by Davy Heder, a Cambodian woman who came to the United States in 1972 after marrying a US soldier, and her friend, Chan Pen Wongbah, who brings a Thai heritage to the storefront restaurant they opened together in the late 1990s. Heder's sister and niece work in the business, along with Wongbah's sister. ❖ The restaurant focuses on both Cambodian and Thai food — two cuisines that emphasize healthy, fresh herbs and vegetables with little oil involved in the cooking. Ginger, lemon grass, mint, and scallions are ubiquitous. But the Thai food tends to be spicier than its Cambodian cousin. The dining room also reflects both cultures, with Cambodian and Thai art on the walls. The vibe is casual and can get noisy on weekends. In good weather, try to snag a seat on the back patio.
❖ Start with the nem chhaw ($6.50), a fresh spring roll with sprouts, cilantro, Asian mint, carrot, basil, chopped lettuce, fine noodles, and minced shrimp. It comes with a creamy peanut sauce studded with toasted sesame seeds. ❖ The Mekong calamari ($5.50) is a small plate of tender rings, lightly breaded, with a sweet chili sauce — tasty but not outstanding. Pad thai is the Caesar salad of Thai food, the staple on every menu. When it's good, it's very good, but when it's bad, it's limp and flavorless. Here it excels. We love the southern pad thai ($10.95 with shrimp, $9.95 with tofu or chicken), an occasional special in which a dash of curry powder livens things up. Another variation is the crispy pad ($9.95), in which the noodles are deep-fried. ❖ The chili duck ($15.95) was a unanimous hit, stir-fried with veggies galore. Broccoli, mushrooms, carrots, baby corn, pineapple, zucchini, and cashews abounded in a sweet-and-sour sauce. ❖ The only weak note was the saraman ($14.95 with steak or shrimp, $12.95 chicken or tofu). We opted for the steak; the meat was chewy, though the coconut curry sauce nicely complemented the chunks of pineapple. A better bet is the emerald salmon ($15.95), an occasional special. The grilled fillet is topped with homemade green curry and coconut milk sauce. Broccoli, squash, and carrots accompany the dish, with white or brown rice. ❖ We love the coconut, ginger, and green tea ice cream ($4.25), but a special treat is vanilla ice cream deep-fried and drizzled with a honey sauce ($4.25). It's a delicious ending to a fine meal that will leave you sated and solvent.

BELLA ENGLISH, *Globe Staff*

# Saray Restaurant

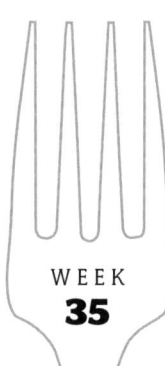

WEEK **35**

1098 Commonwealth Ave., Boston
617-383-6651

www.sarayboston.com

MasterCard and Visa accepted.

Restrooms not accessible.

**PRICES** Appetizers, soups, salads: $3.95-$18.95. Entrees: $13.95-$22.95. Desserts: $3.50-$6.95.

**HOURS** Daily 11 a.m.-11 p.m.

**ALCOHOL** None.

### HEY, TRY THESE

White bean salad, eggplant salad, red lentil soup, zucchini pancakes, palace-style pastrami.

**TASTING NOTES**

BOSTON · CAMBRIDGE

**THIS TURKISH RESTAURANT** is sweet and welcoming and the food remarkable — and totally authentic. ❖ The owners are Selahaattin Ercisli from Van, in the eastern part of Turkey, and Omer Kara from Istanbul, who has lived here for 13 years. Kara also owns Cooking Cafe next door. ❖ Here, Turkish cooking is dressed up (saray means "palace"); tables are cloth-covered; flatware is slipped into the folds of apricot-colored napkins. Some of Saray's items are over the $15 Cheap Eats limit (including all of the seafood), but that leaves many kebabs and an array of little dishes. ❖ Lamb meat soup ($4.95) reminds me of a bowl made with sheep's head that I didn't have the guts to order in Morocco. It comes with a shot of vinegar studded with chopped garlic. Our waitress advises tipping the vinegar into the soup. The broth is intensely lamb-y. ❖ Less challenging is the famous red lentil soup with mint ($3.95), a cheery orange bowl with a bright herby taste. A generous mound of plump white beans make a beautiful salad with red onions and tomatoes ($4.95 and $6.95). Delicious home-cured pastrami ($8.95) is grilled in foil on a bed of tomatoes and peppers. Mildly smoky baba ghanouj ($4.50) has only a hint of tahini. Another eggplant salad ($4.50) consists simply of the char-grilled puree, bell peppers, parsley, and olive oil. Both come in three mounds, garnished with succulent oil-cured olives and strawberries(!). Not sure what those are doing on the plate. ❖ Garlicky yogurt sauce blankets one side of a plate of tender lamb-filled cabbage rolls ($12.95); the other half of the plate boasts a bright, barely cooked tomato sauce. Turkey's popular adana kebab ($13.95) consists of two long rolls of ground lamb slipped off their skewers surrounding a mound of long-grain white rice. On the side are an intensely colored red sauerkraut, made with vinegar, salt, and sugar; a dish of pickled green tomatoes, green cabbage, carrots, and other vegetables; shoestrings of red onion bathed in vinegar and parsley; a grilled tomato; and a long, pleasingly hot green pepper. Every sharp taste balances the smoky meat. ❖ The chefs watch us from a large window that looks into the dining room. They send out syrupy walnut and pistachio baklava with a luscious spoonful of sweetened cream. We drink strong Turkish coffee, wishing someone could read the grounds for us, the way a Turkish woman did for me many years ago — and brought good news. ❖ If you read the chefs' coffee grounds, their squiggles and swirls would surely spell success.

SHERYL JULIAN, *Globe Staff*

# Cafe Bistro

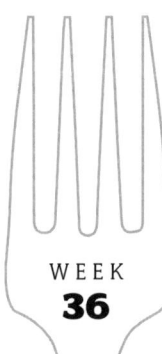

WEEK **36**

*Nordstrom, the Natick Collection,
290 Speen St., Natick
508-318-2600, ext. 1610
www.nordstrom.com
All major credit cards accepted.
Wheelchair accessible.*
**PRICES** *$3.50-$16.95.*
**HOURS** *Mon-Sat 10 a.m.-8 p.m.,
Sun 11 a.m.-5 p.m.*
**ALCOHOL** *Beer and wine.*

### HEY, TRY THESE

Crab bisque, blue cheese-pear salad, roast sirloin ciabatta, roast chicken pommes frites, wild mushroom-herb ricotta pizza, white chocolate bread pudding.

**TASTING NOTES**

_____
_____
_____
_____

BOSTON • CAMBRIDGE

**I CAN SCARCELY AFFORD** to even window-shop at Nordstrom. But I have discovered something there that, happily, falls within my budget: the vaunted store's Cafe Bistro. Here, you can get a cup of soup for $3.50, and the most expensive thing on the menu is the steak pommes frites for $16.95. Most dishes hover between $9 and $12. ❖ Our party of four waited for 15 minutes on a recent Saturday afternoon. Take your husband, or boyfriend, and he can hold your place in line while you scope out the merchandise that surrounds the second-floor restaurant. If you're shopping with kids — I feel for you — there's a place to park the stroller and a separate menu with the usual suspects: pizza, hot dogs, chicken fingers, and such.
❖ The spacious restaurant is pretty, with cherry paneling, banquettes and tables, chic lighting, and translucent shades. High ceilings and carpet keep the noise level down. ❖ Best of all, the food is really tasty, well-prepared and -presented. Start with the crab bisque (cup $4.50, bowl $5.95), a creamy but not-too-heavy rendition with a decent amount of crabmeat.
❖ A blue cheese and pear salad ($9.50) is an entree-size plate of organic mixed greens tossed with warm and tender pear slices, dried cherries, a generous scattering of cheese and candied pecans, and a cherry balsamic vinaigrette. ❖ The restaurant offers a couple of weekly specials, and our resident vegetarian was very pleased with the roasted vegetable panini ($10.95) served on artisan bread. ❖ The roast sirloin ciabatta ($10.25) is a winner. I loved the roast chicken pommes frites ($13.50), an organic, tender breast pounded flat, its skin crisp with herbs. ❖ A large brick oven turns out pizzas: Try the wild mushroom and herb ricotta ($9.50). The crust is yeasty and puffy at the edges but thin and crisp underneath a layer of mushrooms, roasted garlic, and caramelized onion. It's baked with four cheeses and has ribbons of fresh basil on top. ❖ Of the four desserts on the menu, the only disappointment is the chocolate paradise cake ($5.95), which is way too dry despite. The creme brulee ($4.95) is satiny, baked with fresh vanilla beans and topped with fresh raspberries. The cheesecake ($4.95) is respectable. But the white chocolate bread pudding ($5.95) is the clear favorite, an eggy bread concoction served warm in a splash of white chocolate and raspberry sauce.
❖ The service here is professional and efficient, perhaps a bit too efficient. They clearly want to keep the traffic flowing.
❖ When we left at 2:45 p.m., there was still a line, and we could see why.

BELLA ENGLISH, *Globe Staff*

# Rio Brazilian Barbeque

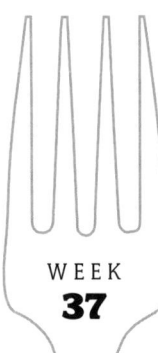

*473 Massachusetts Ave., Arlington*
*781-483-3063*
*www.riobarbq.com*
*All major credit cards accepted.*
*Wheelchair accessible.*

**PRICES** *Entrees/sandwiches/salads: $7.95-$19.95. Self-serve buffet: $9.95-$15.95/person or $5.95/lb). Tableside barbecue, including buffet: $15.95-$21.95.*

**HOURS** *Mon-Fri 5 p.m.-10 p.m., Sat-Sun noon-10 p.m.*

**ALCOHOL** *Beer and wine.*

### HEY, TRY THESE

Shrimp bobo, rodizio churrasco (tableside barbecue), passion fruit mousse, Amazones chai.

TASTING NOTES

WEEK 37

BOSTON • CAMBRIDGE

**MOST OF THE BRAZILIAN** restaurants around Boston — and there are many of them — specialize in self-service buffets selling food by the pound and nonstop barbecues with skewered meats delivered to your table and sliced straight onto your plate. Rio Brazilian Barbeque proves that elegance and Brazilian dining are not mutually exclusive. ❖ Opened by the owners of Punjab, an Indian restaurant a few doors away, Rio breaks the cafeteria mold. Its floors are handsome hardwood, its tables classy marble, its walls richly colorful. At the rear of the dining room, the restaurant's rotisserie grill is on full, flaming display. ❖ The all-you-can-eat or pay-by-the-pound buffet is artfully separated from the dining room by a rippled glass divider. And its rodizio churrasco service is surprisingly ambitious for a 50-seat place. Ten different meats cycle round the room, including lamb, sirloin, beef ribs, chicken hearts, pork loin, and three types of sausage (beef, chicken, and kielbasa). ❖ The buffet ($5.95/pound takeout, $6.95/pound meats-only, all-you-can-eat lunch $9.95, all-you-can-eat dinner $15.95) is the main reason I've visited again and again. It's perfect for any appetite or schedule, whether you want a small take-out container of beef meatballs, a scoop of chunky chicken salad sweetened with raisins and topped with crunchy potato sticks, or a heaping sit-down meal of white rice, black beans, fried plantains, diced beets tossed with capers, shredded collard greens, garlicky zucchini, chicken thighs with green peas, lean boneless pork, creamy chicken lasagna, and more. ❖ Buffet rights also come with the rodizio ($15.95 lunch, $21.95 dinner). Most of the meats are minimally seasoned but get intense flavor from the caramelized crusts that form as they slow-roast over the fire. The rodizio's highlights are perfectly moist pork, tender sirloin that explodes with bold taste, and beef ribs that release their rich flavor slowly as you chew. Lamb, bacon-wrapped chicken, and chicken sausage are a touch dry, but oily beef sausage bursts with spicy flair. ❖ If self-control isn't your strong point, you can limit your food intake by ordering a dinner entree, including shrimp (or tofu) bobo ($15.95), a starchy, soupy mixture of mashed yucca, tomatoes, onions, and cilantro served in a clay pot, and cabrito gomes ($18.95), a bone-in stew of gamy, tough-but-flavorful Guinness-marinated goat with minted rice and fried garlic. ❖ Skip the flan ($5.95). The dessert to order is the passion fruit mousse ($5.95), which packs a sweet, tart punch with every creamy spoonful. It's best washed down with Amazones chai ($2.50), a wide mug of milky, spicy tea served with the charming extra touch of stirring sticks coated in sugar.

SACHA PFEIFFER, *Globe Staff*

# Kitchen on Common

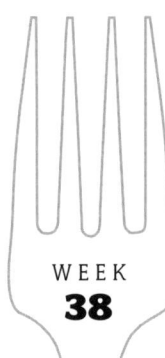

WEEK **38**

442 Common St., Cushing Square, Belmont
617-484-4328
*www.kitchenoncommon.com*
All major credit cards accepted.
Wheelchair accessible.
**PRICES** Appetizers: $5. Entrees: $12-$15. Dessert: $1.50-$2.50.
**HOURS** Mon-Sat 11:30 a.m.-8:30 p.m.
**ALCOHOL** No liquor license, but you may bring your own.

## HEY, TRY THESE

Sausage and kale soup, baby spinach salad with pancetta, grilled pork loin with brioche bread pudding, braised chicken stew with Parmesan polenta, grilled salmon with oyster mushroom and potato hash. (Menu changes seasonally.)

**TASTING NOTES**
_____
_____
_____
_____
_____

BOSTON • CAMBRIDGE

**EVERY ONCE IN A WHILE,** a chef comes along who is all the right things: earnest, modest, and talented. This describes Joh Kokubo to a T. ❖ He was raised in Lexington, worked at the Franklin Cafe, went to the French Culinary Institute in New York, and returned to this area to work while he thought about opening his own place. ❖ On the phone from his 16-seat Kitchen on Common, Kokubo, who is half Japanese, talks about establishing relationships with local farmers and how he found Gretta Anderson, who has a Community Supported Agriculture winter program in Belmont that's supplying him with vegetables. From another chef, he picked up the tip of cutting a boneless pork chop horizontally so the two halves cook more quickly. And in a previous job, he discovered that he could make a big batch of polenta right before service and spoon the rich golden mixture beside main courses as he needed it. ❖ Kokubo, 33, is sending out terrific food to his small, cheerful dining room. Every morsel on every plate is homemade, sourced carefully, and well thought out. ❖ Kokubo has a pared-down menu of five appetizers and five entrees. His wife, Annette Saulsbury, 31, who works as a private chef and helps out, makes splendid old-fashioned cookie-jar cookies ($1.50 each) and one dessert. One day, that's an apple turnover ($2.50), which the chef takes time to warm through, so the flaky pastry and aromatic fruits are at their best. ❖ Sausage and kale soup ($5) arrives in a huge bowl, though the portion isn't large. Sweet crumbled meat, chopped greens, and thinly sliced fingerling potatoes make a satisfying broth. Curly red lettuce leaves are the greens of the day ($5), with the clever kohlrabi slaw as the garnish. ❖ The chef's grilled pork loin, with its caramelized edges and faintly pink meat, is accompanied by a square of brioche bread pudding ($15) and sautéed apples and leeks. A chicken stew, flecked with butternut squash and white beans, is too dry one night, and ideally moist another. But the polenta is smooth and beautiful on both occasions. ❖ Beside moist salmon that had been grilled ($14) sat a delightful hash of oyster mushrooms, leeks, and potatoes. Among the sides ($4 each) are faintly sweet roasted carrots with maple syrup, herby mushrooms, and roasted beets with braised kale. ❖ Kitchen on Common has no liquor license, so we brought wine and sipped it from water glasses, lingering longer than we should have. But we were the only customers in the house.❖ That will never happen again.

SHERYL JULIAN, *Globe Staff*

# Viet Grill

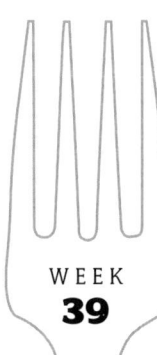

645 Washington St., Canton
781-828-3058
Cash only. One step up for wheelchairs.
**PRICES** *$3-$9.95.*
**HOURS** *Tue-Fri 11:30 a.m.-10 p.m., Sat-Sun noon-10 p.m. Closed Mon.*
**ALCOHOL** *None.*

WEEK **39**

## HEY, TRY THESE

Vietnamese salad, spring rolls, pho, grilled chicken, chicken or beef sate, Vietnamese patties, Vietnamese crepe, bun, Vietnamese homemade custard.

**TASTING NOTES**

**TWO THINGS YOU SHOULD KNOW** before you go to the Viet Grill: Take cash and bring your own beer or wine. Then settle in for a wonderfully fresh and creative meal. We hesitate to call the service slow since that's a pejorative in the restaurant world. But even chef/owner Tan Doan will tell you that "sometimes, people have to wait." That's because everything is cooked to order. ❖ The new Viet Grill has a small, plain dining room, with just seven tables. A good start is the Vietnamese salad ($4.75), a healthy and colorful medley of carrots and cabbage marinated in lemon sugar and topped with crushed peanuts and cilantro. There's a sweet dressing enlivened with some red pepper. ❖ Though children are sometimes reluctant to try ethnic foods, the ones in our party loved the hand-squeezed lemonade ($1.95) and the beef and chicken sate ($6.75). These succulent skewers of meat with a sweet glaze are served with a side of peanut sauce and a warm noodle salad. ❖ A staple of Vietnamese restaurants, the pho — or soup — here manages to be both delicate and hearty. There's chicken or beef, a large bowl for $6. With generous amounts of shredded meat, the soup has thin strands of vermicelli at the bottom and a sprinkling of cilantro on top. ❖ A table favorite was the grilled quarter-chicken with lemongrass ($6.75). The chicken is delectable and crisp. Try the Vietnamese patties ($7.95), little cakes of ground shrimp, chicken, and pork with carrots, onions, and scallions, steamed and served over a bed of vermicelli and vegetables with a garlicky dipping sauce on the side. One of my favorite Vietnamese dishes is bun, or a vermicelli bowl filled with bean sprouts, carrots, and a choice of marinated beef, chicken, or pork. There's also a choice of cut-up spring rolls on top of the noodles ($6.50), with the usual veggies and a lively sauce. It's a one-bowl meal, and the crunchy rolls offer a nice contrast to the tender noodles. We didn't love the salmon grilled in banana leaves ($9.75), which was a little tough and chewy. ❖ Leave room for the only dessert: Vietnamese homemade custard ($3), a sweet flan. ❖ Doan learned to cook from his parents, who owned a restaurant in South Vietnam. He fled the country after the war, met his wife Gam Nguyen here; and together, they've run nine restaurants. Not long ago, they moved back to Vietnam. "But it was very different. It was not totally free. We missed America," he says. ❖ For our selfish sakes, we're glad they did.

BELLA ENGLISH, *Globe Staff*

# El Pelon Taqueria

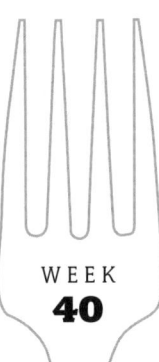

WEEK **40**

92 Peterborough St., Boston (Fenway)
617-262-9090
www.elpelon.com
Major credit cards except Discover accepted.
Fully accessible.
**PRICES** $2.50-$15.95.
**HOURS** Tue-Sun noon-10 p.m.
**ALCOHOL** None.

### HEY, TRY THESE

Quesadilla, grilled chicken torta, cheese enchilada with green mole.

**TASTING NOTES**
_____
_____
_____
_____

*Mex*

**BOSTON • CAMBRIDGE**

**THE BLOCK OF LITTLE RESTAURANTS** and storefronts in The Fenway, where El Pelon Taqueria is located, is so lively it will make you envy the people who get to live there. ❖ El Pelon, a tiny gem of a place with 16 seats inside and another 16 on picnic benches outside, came into this neighborhood several years ago, and its Mexican food has been a big hit ever since. The grilled chicken sandwich with refried beans, limey onions, and a chili-spiked mayonnaise ($4.85) is worth the price — and the parking ticket. You see, The Fenway neighbors seem to have reserved all the parking spaces for themselves, and the police enforce the residents-only rule. So don't take their spaces and gamble that you'll get away with it. There are meters up and down Boylston Street and Brookline Avenue, and they'll only cost you a bit of a walk. And don't go if there's a game in town, unless of course you're going to the game. ❖ That settled, begin with chef/owner Nathaniel Walker's quesadilla ($2.85) filled with a local Jack cheese. The hot quesadilla is pulled off the grill and the outside is sprinkled with salt. ❖ Everything at El Pelon comes served on foil trays or paper baskets, or wrapped in foil. And no napkins are sturdy enough for these morsels — especially the voluptuous burritos — so you need to begin with a wad. But the menu is so cheap (the most expensive item is $6.50), you'll forgive all this. ❖ Torta is the name of a Mexican sandwich, prepared on a toasted roll heaped with refried beans, onions marinated in lime, and guacamole. Add anything to that — braised pork, grilled chicken, grilled steak (all $4.85) — and you end up with something that will make you immensely happy. ❖ Cheese enchilada with green mole sauce ($3.75) doesn't look like much, sort of flat in its little foil tray, but the salty white Mexican cheese, with Jack and goat cheese mixed in, will surprise you, and so will the cumin-scented tomatilla mole with roasted garlic, pumpkin seeds, and cinnamon. ❖ Alas, there's no beer here (which the food begs for), but you can wash it down with horchata ($1.50), a dairy free, milky looking drink made by soaking ground rice, almonds, and cinnamon in hot water.

SHERYL JULIAN, *Globe Correspondent*

# Good Food Cafe

*2378 Massachusetts Ave., Cambridge*
*617-876-2450.*
*www.jimsgoodfood.com*
*Visa and MasterCard accepted. Wheelchair accessible.*

**PRICES** *$3.25-$6.75.*

**HOURS** *Tue-Sat 8 a.m.-9 p.m. Sun 10 a.m.-6 p.m.*

**ALCOHOL** *None.*

WEEK **41**

### HEY, TRY THESE

Egg sandwich with tomatoes and blue cheese; roasted turkey, stuffing, and cranberry sauce sandwich; meatball sandwich; reuben; fresh mozzarella, pesto, and roasted red pepper sandwich; Elvis smoothie.

TASTING NOTES

_____
_____
_____
_____

BOSTON · CAMBRIDGE

**I CONFESS TO SUSPECTING** that Jim Walsh was creatively challenged when I first heard the name of his new North Cambridge restaurant: the Good Food Cafe. But I underestimated how genuine the moniker was intended to be.

❖ Breaking the typical sub shop mold, Walsh roasts his own chicken and turkey, makes his own meatballs, blends his own salad dressings and pesto, and does much of his own baking. He uses Iggy's breads, puts fresh-grated nutmeg in his cookies and muffins, and mellows out the vinegary bite of store-bought roasted red peppers by soaking them in homemade sweet marinade. His menu is limited — about a dozen sandwiches, a half-dozen salads, and a daily soup, plus baked goods and drinks — but he keeps quality high by maintaining a narrow focus. ❖ He also brings unexpected pizzazz to his cooking. Egg sandwiches ($2.25-$4.40), served until noon, are made with sliced hard-boiled eggs, grilled on a press, and dressed up with more than just bacon. If you like, he'll add prosciutto, pesto, spicy mayo, or, my favorite, an inspired pairing of tomatoes and savory blue cheese ($3.20). ❖ Walsh takes the time to dry bread crumbs for the stuffing, redolent with sage, in his roasted turkey sandwich with cranberry sauce ($6.50), just as he mixes beef, basil, eggs, and bread for his tender meatball sandwich ($5.50), topped with marinara and melted provolone. ❖ A butter-brushed Reuben ($6.25) is piled with exceptionally lean corned beef. A simple garden salad ($4.50) is a generous mix of beautiful greens, cukes, red peppers, and carrot slivers. The house-made dressings are very nice. The Elvis smoothie ($3.25 large, $2.75 small) — a full-bodied blend of milk, peanut butter, and banana — is rich enough to be dessert. ❖ A few items falter. Caesar salad ($4.50, with chicken $6.25) comes buried in an unappetizing heap of tasteless, powdery parmesan cheese. Chicken soups ($4.25) are made with dark thigh meat, not the white breast meat many health-conscious customers prefer. And Walsh isn't likely to win awards for his baking; his cookies ($1.50) are oddly flat and pale, his muffins ($1.75) have strangely wet tops. ❖ He does have a flair for interior design, though. High-ceilinged, cavernous, and wood-floored, the cafe's space feels bare and empty, even with table seating for 20 scattered around. But work by local artists adorn the walls, two funky red leather couches fill one corner, a magazine-strewn coffee table encourages customers to stay awhile, and happy paint colors — bright orange, electric green — add warmth and good cheer. ❖ It's a sunny setting for some truly good food.

SACHA PFEIFFER, *Globe Staff*

# Pescatore Seafood

WEEK **42**

158 Boston Ave., Ball Square, Somerville
617-623-0003
www.pescatoreseafood.com
Cash only. Wheelchair accessible.
**PRICES** $3.95-$16.95 (most items under $15).
**HOURS** Sat-Sun 4-10 p.m.,
Tue-Fri 11 a.m.-10 p.m. Closed Mon.
**ALCOHOL** Beer and wine.

### HEY, TRY THESE

Fried calamari, fusilli Amalfi, grilled salmon, ravioli, tiramisu.

**TASTING NOTES**

BOSTON • CAMBRIDGE

**THE PHRASE "HIDDEN TREASURE"** is too often used to describe places that really aren't, but in the case of Pescatore Seafood, it's absolutely accurate. ❖ For one thing, Pescatore is hidden — at the less-traveled edge of Somerville's Ball Square, tucked behind Kelly's Diner. The dining room is a lovely, calm area with a touch of sophisticated restraint — a lot like the food that's served there. ❖ Pescatore (which means "fisherman" in Italian) specializes in seafood, and that's mostly what we stuck to. A fried calamari appetizer ($10.95) of golden rings and tentacles, served with a fresh, light marinara dipping sauce, showed that someone in Pescatore's kitchen has a sure hand with a fryolator. These calamari were tender and sweet, and the coating was perfectly crispy. ❖ Anna Buonopane, who is from Gaeta, on the Mediterranean coast of Italy's boot, owns Pescatore with her husband, Luigi. She uses several different seafood purveyors, looking for the freshest catch. The grilled salmon ($16.95) was beautifully cooked, nicely crisped outside but tender and moist inside. The dish came with a generous helping of vegetables — some of the best I've had at a restaurant. ❖ The fusilli was so good it made our eyes roll with delight. Buonopane makes it herself, along with the fettuccini and ravioli: That pasta alone would keep me coming back. We tried the fusilli Amalfi ($16.95) with shrimp, scallops, and lobster meat, and the light, slightly tangy garlic, oil, and white wine sauce was a perfect complement to the dense, al dente fusilli. The scallops were bland, but the lobster meat was sweet and succulent. The sautéed broccoli rabe served with it was also apparently quite good, but it was gobbled up before I could taste it. ❖ The squash-filled ravioli in marsala sauce had our eyes rolling happily again. The pasta was firm but soft, and the squash filling, slightly sweetened with amaretti cookies, was nicely complemented by the sweetness of the sauce.

❖ There are five desserts on the menu: creme caramel, tiramisu, pastiera, gelato, and sorbet. Buonopane makes the sorbet ($5.95) using seasonal fruit and whisks in Italian mascarpone at the end. I actually preferred the tiramisu ($5.95) because it was lighter (sounds crazy, I know). Buonopane also makes the tiramisu, and it's great, with soft but distinct layers of lady fingers, a velvety texture from the mascarpone, and a strong coffee liqueur flavor.

ANN LUISA CORTISSOZ, *Globe Staff*

# Brown Sugar Cafe

WEEK **43**

*129 Jersey St., Boston (Fenway)*
*617-266-2928*
*www.brownsugarcafe.com*
*Visa, MasterCard, Diner's Club accepted.*
*Fully accessible.*

**PRICES** *Lunch: $3.95-$10.50. Dinner: $3.95-$20.95 (most dishes don't exceed $15.95).*

**HOURS** *Mon-Thu 11 a.m.-10 p.m., Fri 11 a.m.-11 p.m., Sat noon-11 p.m., Sun noon-10 p.m*

**ALCOHOL** *Full bar.*

### HEY, TRY THESE

Vegetable tempura, tod mun (ground shrimp fritters), yum nua (grilled beef salad), pad Thai country—style, coffee custard.

TASTING NOTES

BOSTON • CAMBRIDGE

**BEST TO DEAL** with the location first. The original Brown Sugar Cafe is on Jersey Street, which is off Boylston opposite Yawkey Way (listen up baseball fans). If you miss it, you'll get lost in the Fenway and drive around forever. Parking is horrendous; it's all for residents, though Jersey Street does have some visitor spaces. ❖ Location aside, though, Suriyant "Toy" Jamdee and his partner, Suraphong "Tu" Pinyochon (the cooking part of the team), and Pinyochon's wife, Darny, years ago created a Cheap Eats classic that endures, and it doesn't look a bit low-budget. They chose the name Brown Sugar Cafe because it's a popular name in Thailand, where raw brown sugar is a common ingredient in cooking. Later, they opened a second location at 1033 Commonwealth Ave. ❖ Given that they are in Boston, the partners take some liberties with the food. Their vegetable tempura ($6.95), for instance, is crisp and light, made with vegetables that Thai cooks ordinary don't use — zucchini, cauliflower red and green bell peppers, sweet potato. The tod mun, ground shrimp fritters ($6.95), are heavenly, made in the traditional Thai style with aromatic spices. ❖ Yum nua, grilled beef salad ($12.95), is hot, crunchy, cooling, and good. It consists of grilled tenderloin with a spicy lemon dressing on a bed of lettuce, cucumbers, and tomatoes. You taste the heat only after a bite or two. ❖ Not everything on this menu is unusual. The red curry (beef, chicken, pork or tofu, $11.95; shrimp or duck, $13.95) is pleasingly hot and not sweet like some curries. Pad Thai country-style (chicken and shrimp or chicken only, $10.95; shrimp only, $12.95) is billed as "a truly native dish." It begins with pad Thai. Spiced tofu is added to the basic dish, as are turnips preserved in salt and sugar. ❖ Brown sugar mango fried rice (chicken & shrimp or chicken only, $13.95; shrimp only, $15.95) is made with brown, rather than white, rice. This adds an unexpected nuttiness, which goes well with the chicken and shrimp. Some food has a little kick, as in BBQ seafood ($15.95), a dish of charcoal grilled squid, shrimp, scallops and fish in a chili sauce. ❖ If you like strong coffee, try the Thai coffee custard ($5.50), which is a creme caramel surrounded with dark coffee syrup. ❖ During baseball season, Brown Sugar Cafe is well positioned for supper before the game. On those nights when the restaurant is jam-packed, it may put a crimp in Jamdee's remarkable memory for recalling what customers ordered previously. But at this point, fans don't fluster this team.

SHERYL JULIAN, *Globe Staff*

# Taso's Euro-Cafe

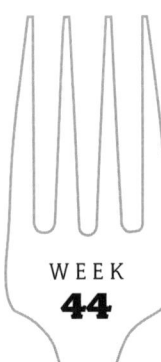

WEEK **44**

*125 Access Road, Norwood (at the Norwood Airport)*
*781-278-0001*
*www.tasoseurocafe.com*
*All major credit cards accepted. Wheelchair accessible.*

**PRICES** *$3.95-$13.95.*
**HOURS** *Mon-Fri 11 a.m.-9 p.m., Sat 7 a.m.-9 p.m.*
**ALCOHOL** *None.*

### HEY, TRY THESE

Tzatziki dip, stuffed grape leaves, pastichio, spinach pie, baked lamb, American chop suey, gyros, souvlaki, pizza, baklava, kataifi, milfae, biscotti.

**TASTING NOTES**

**SIX AND A HALF YEARS AGO,** I wrote a glowing Cheap Eats review on Taso's Euro-Cafe, then located in Quincy. Three weeks later, the place was destroyed by a fire. For all these years I've wondered what happened to the family that ran Taso's — and I wondered when I would ever find another Greek restaurant to match it. ❖ Happily, both questions have been answered. Taso Kapsaskis and his cafe resurfaced in an unlikely spot — the Norwood Airport. Everything here is made from scratch. ❖ Start with a plate-size Greek salad ($5.95); the homemade dressing is tart and tangy. Kapsaskis calls the horiatiki ($8.95) "the real Greek salad." It comes with warm rolls to dip into the pungent olive oil. ❖ For a snack, try the stuffed grape leaves ($6.95) cooked in olive oil and lemon juice and filled with rice and herbs. We also love the creamy tzatziki dip ($5.95), which is served with toasted pita triangles and made with robust Greek yogurt, diced cucumbers, garlic, olive oil, and red wine vinegar. I would have been happy eating a bowl of this and nothing else. ❖ The pastichio ($9.95) may be my favorite thing here. It's the Greek version of lasagna, with long, tubular pasta from Greece, ground beef, and tomato sauce, all topped by an inch of fluffy béchamel sauce.

❖ Everything here is seasoned just right. Kapsaskis uses Greek salt from his wife's hometown, and Greek mountain oregano, said to be among the world's most fragrant. It's perfect for the kebabs and lamb dishes that Taso's does so well. ❖ Souvlaki is the original Greek meal; here it's chicken ($10.95) or lamb ($12.95), the grilled chunks of meat alternating on skewers with slightly charred onions and peppers. Taso's Famous Baked Lamb ($12.95), offered Thursday through Saturday, lives up to its billing. He roasts slabs of lamb shanks and simmers them in a heady tomato sauce with a touch of cinnamon and nutmeg and a dash of retsina to bring out the flavor. ❖ I'm running out of space here, and there's so much more. Greek iced coffee frappe ($2.95): smooth, frothy, strong. Gyros ($5.95-$8.95): lamb and beef cooked on a rotisserie, stuffed into a pita wrap with veggies and tzatziki dip. Spinach pie ($6.95 appetizer, $9.95 dinner): creamy spinach and feta cheese, onions, and herbs baked in layers of crisp filo. ❖ Maroula, Taso's wife, does the desserts. You won't find better baklava, kataifi, milfae, cookies, and biscotti (cinnamon, walnut, or plain), all baked daily. The Norwood Airport may not be on your radar screen, but Taso's Euro-Cafe should be.

BELLA ENGLISH, *Globe Staff*

# City Slicker Cafe

WEEK **45**

*588 Somerville Ave., Somerville*
*617-625-0700*
*www.cityslickercafe.com*
*All major credit cards accepted.*
*Not wheelchair accessible (one step up).*
**PRICES** *$5-$15.*
**HOURS** *Tue-Sun 11 a.m.-10:45 p.m.*
**ALCOHOL** *None.*

### HEY, TRY THESE

Roasted eggplant and fresh mozzarella pasta, baked meatballs, chicken piccata, garlic steak tips, Tree Hugger pizza.

**TASTING NOTES**

**DON'T UNDERESTIMATE** the elation people feel when a favorite restaurant rises from the dead. The Urban Gourmet, formerly in Somerville's Ball Square, recently enjoyed such a resurrection; after closing last year due to landlord troubles, its owner, Richard Warren, started a similar restaurant about a mile away. ❖ City Slicker serves the same terrific thin-crust pizzas that made Urban Gourmet locally beloved. They're baked in a pan drizzled with olive oil, and slow-baked at a relatively low temperature. That means you'll wait at least 25 minutes for your pie — but, as a sign by the register promises, patience will be rewarded. That's no lie; our "Tree Hugger" ($9 small/$14 large) — an all-veggie mélange of roasted eggplant, baby spinach, roasted tomatoes, and fresh mozzarella — was the best pizza I've had in recent memory thanks to its standout crust and vibrant flavors. ❖ And although you can order a pepperoni pie, that would be a timid move given the creative combos available. A sampling: Bolognese (ragu, goat cheese, cheddar), City Girl (portobello mushrooms, gorgonzola, caramelized onions); and Steak and Potatoes (garlic steak, roasted potatoes, blue cheese, fried shallots). ❖ But City Slicker isn't content simply to be a pizza joint. ❖ City Slicker offers lots of hearty, cooked-to-order comfort foods, such as meatloaf ($10.50) and pork chops ($11.95). It balances cardiac-unfriendly choices, like deep-fried Panko crab puffs ($7.25), with healthy ones, like whole wheat pasta, fresh fish, and greens usually not found at sub shops (garlic baby spinach, asparagus, broccolini). ❖ The food has flair, too. Pulled pork ($6.85) is simmered in garlic red wine, Portuguese-style; a Cuban sandwich ($7.75) is brightened with citrus mayo; and baked cod ($12.95) is stuffed with crab and pancetta, then finished with lemon parsley beurre blanc. Every eat-in meal begins with house-made focaccia served in a decorative bread basket with red pepper-parmesan olive oil. You can also customize your food with extras like fried shallots, tomato-avocado salsa, and sauces ranging from sesame wasabi to jalapeno vinaigrette. ❖ Chicken-shrimp paella ($12.95) suffered from bland shellfish, but it's a lot of food for the money, and the mixture of brown rice, roasted red peppers, peas, shallots, pink beans, parsley, and garlic had bold taste. ❖ For dessert, there are cream cheese brownies from Winter Hill Bakery and ice cream or sorbet from Christina's. Most of City Slicker's business is take-out, but eating in is pleasant; the dining room has vivid orange walls and funky photographs. There's also a poster of a giant avocado in the window — more proof that this is a pizzeria with loftier ambitions.

SACHA PFEIFFER, *Globe Staff*

# Deluxe Town Diner

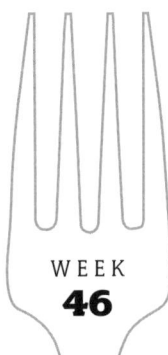

WEEK **46**

*627 Mt. Auburn St., Watertown*
*617-924-9789*
*www.deluxetowndiner.com*
*All major credit cards accepted.*
*Not wheelchair accessible.*
**PRICES** *$1.50-$15.95.*
**HOURS** *Daily 7 a.m.-10 p.m.*
**ALCOHOL** *None.*

### HEY, TRY THESE

French toast, poached eggs, warm spinach salad, crab cakes, grilled curried chicken, fish and chips, roasted half chicken, strawberry shortcake, chocolate bread pudding.

TASTING NOTES
_____
_____
_____
_____

BOSTON • CAMBRIDGE

**DON LEVY COULD HAVE TURNED** the 1940s Town Diner on Watertown's Mount Auburn Street into something so precious that the old-timers in town would have winced at the thought of stopping by. ❖ But he's too stylish to do that. Not Armani stylish. Levy is all Polartec and horn rims. And he has a way with old places, though he says he's a self-trained designer. ❖ Levy, who lives in Watertown, was looking at property to do a shop that specialized in "gourmet hot dogs and cold cuts." Instead, he saw Town Diner and imagined it in all its glory. He practically bought it on impulse. He went about his renovation carefully, kept the best of the old stuff, and unearthed some of the sky-blue tiles with their black trim. ❖ Before you knew it, there were house-made fries are coming out of the Fryolator to be served alongside hamburgers from celebrity purveyor John Dewar, butcher to all the fine restaurants in town. The tea here is loose, the waiters are engaging, and the grill cook, flipping Rhode Island johnnycakes and thick French toast, might be talking on his cell phone. Levy and his crew call this lively place "fine dinering," which makes you think they're having fun. ❖ Town Diner opens at 7 a.m. and offers all the standard breakfast and lunch fare. But people also eat lighter these days, and vegetarians like diners, too. This explains why there are "soy sausages" on the morning menu, and several non-meat lunch and dinner choices as well, including stir-fries, mac and cheese, and tofu burgers. We went for the tofu burger and felt childish heaping both mustard and ketchup on the thing to give it some life (to no avail). But the sweet potato fries were fine, and so were the regular fries with a thick fillet of meaty white fish on a splendid fish and chips plate ($11.50).
❖ Crab cakes were light and mostly crab. They flaked right on the fork. Warm spinach salad ($9.50) was smoky from some extraordinary bacon, generously doused with buttermilk dressing and presented in a large bowl.
❖ Don's wife, Daryl Levy, made two wonderful desserts, both light and pleasing: strawberry shortcake with a yogurt-sour cream garnish and a chocolate bread pudding floating in a cool pool of milk. There are other, richer, cakes and confections, says Levy. Pies, he says, "but no Table Talk."
❖ Some nostalgia is better left as a memory.

SHERYL JULIAN, *Globe Staff*

# Suvarnabhumi Kiri

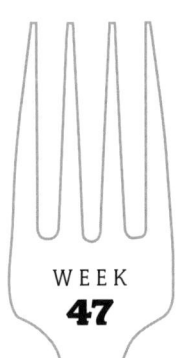

WEEK **47**

*90 Harvard Ave., Allston*
*617-562-8888*
*All major credit cards accepted.*
*Wheelchair accessible.*

**PRICES** *$8.95-$14.95 (more for sushi platters).*
**HOURS** *Mon-Thu 11:30 a.m.-3:30 p.m. and 4:30-10:30 p.m., Fri until 11 p.m., Sat noon-11 p.m., Sun 5-10:30 p.m.*
**ALCOHOL** *None.*

## HEY, TRY THESE

Prahok katee (veggies and spicy pork dip), Thai Siam nuggets, mouan ang (Cambodian-style satay), Thai chicken satay, Grapow maki roll, s'nao namgnou (Cambodian tangy chicken soup), tom ka kai (Thai coconut soup), samlor machu yuon (sweet and sour stew), loc lac (caramelized beef), samlor kako (curry stew), pork grapow (spicy pork), mango with sticky rice, fresh lychee on ice, green tea ice cream.

TASTING NOTES

BOSTON · CAMBRIDGE

**LET THE LOVERS OF THAT STINKY,** gray, gloppy fish paste called prahok rejoice. Boston (well, Allston) has a new Cambodian restaurant, and it's not afraid to use this odorous but tasty Cambodian foodstuff that all adventurous eaters should try.

❖ But those looking for more familiar flavors need not shy away. Suvarnabhumi Kiri also offers an epic selection of sushi and Thai in a pretty space with a reasonable beer, wine, and sake list. ❖ When we settled into the spacious dining room dotted with dark, glossy tables, we flipped past the Thai and sushi pages and headed to the back of the menu. There we found about two dozen Cambodian choices, and it turns out there's more to come. ❖ We went straight for the prahok. This fermented fish is used as a seasoning in Cambodia. The paste was in its full glory in the prahok katee ($12.95), adding a rich, salty undertone to this spicy dip of ground pork, creamy coconut milk, tasty Thai basil, and intensely aromatic Kaffir lime leaves. The dip was ringed by crisp, fresh vegetables, and we couldn't stop dipping. It's an entree, but it's more fun as a shared appetizer. ❖ Three soups proved the Khmer cooks in the kitchen (who work alongside the Thai cooks) really know how to brew and stew. Cambodian chicken soup (s'nao namgnou, $4.25) looked like a simple broth flecked with scallion and lime leaf, but one sip revealed a seemingly endless roll call of flavors. The cook seasons this soup by the cup, smashing and swishing lemongrass, cilantro-like sawtooth herb, Asian mint, and more in the broth before scooping it all out. ❖ A delicate sweet and sour stew (somlar machu youn, best with shrimp, $10.95) — swimming with crunchy lotus root, soft chunks of papaya, and toasty fried garlic — also had a complex, addictive broth. A thick garden stew (samlor kako, $12.95) with chicken was a tasty tangle of spinach, beans, Asian pumpkin, and squash in a dusky, prahok-tweaked brew. ❖ Other Khmer classics, such as juicy beef loc lac ($11.95), and a light, homemade, green curry (samlor katee, $12.95) tossed over super-fresh vegetables, were just as satisfying. ❖ Meanwhile, a brief sampling of the Thai and sushi menus turned up some very good Thai and some gorgeous but average-tasting sushi that we expect will improve under the guidance of co-owner Nathan Chhour, who spent 10 years as a sushi chef at Jae's Cafe. ❖ But it's the Cambodian flavors that got us most excited, because life's simply too short for yet another plate of pad Thai.

DENISE TAYLOR, *Globe Correspondent*

# Lorenz Island Kuisine

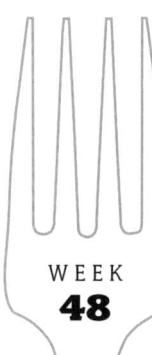

WEEK **48**

*657 Washington St., Dorchester*
*617-506-6061*
*www.lorenzislandkuisine.com*
*All major credit cards accepted.*
*Wheelchair accessible.*
**PRICES** *$1.50-$12.75*
**HOURS** *Mon-Wed 8 a.m.-10 p.m., Thu-Fri 8 a.m.-midnight, Sat 9 a.m.-midnight, Sun 10 a.m.-7 p.m.*
**ALCOHOL** *Beer and wine.*

### HEY, TRY THESE

Beef and chicken patties, jerk chicken, curry chicken, curry goat, oxtail stew, frosted fruit cake.

TASTING NOTES

**THERE'S REGGAE ON THE RADIO,** coconut water in the cooler, and chicken patties under the heat lamp. Lorenz Island Kuisine, with its bright walls and friendly owners, is a welcoming spot serving authentic Jamaican food in Codman Square. Chris Lorenz Graham owns the place and runs it along with his wife, Samantha, and sister, Michelle. The siblings were born in Jamaica and learned to cook at the knee of a master: their mother. ❖ "She's still the best cook I know," Chris says. As if on cue, his mother, Cynthia, walks in, and checks on the desserts. She supplies the restaurant with her specialties several times a week. A kindergarten teacher, her passion is baking, and she does wedding and special-occasion cakes on the side.
❖ The menu here is straightforward, and you can get breakfast, lunch, or dinner. On weekend nights, the crowd can go downstairs for music and dancing. ❖ Except for the two fish dishes, the entrees come in three sizes and are the same price ($5.50, $7.49, $8.99): each comes with rice or roti skin, and a choice of sides such as plantains, rice and peas, dumplings, mac and cheese, and johnny cake. ❖ No Jamaican feast is complete without jerk chicken. Ask for the sauce on the side, though; it will light you up. There's a nice, spicy rub that makes the skin crisp while the chicken falls off the bone. The rice contains red beans and chopped pork, and the callaloo we've ordered as a side reminds us of a sweeter version of collard greens, flecked with bits of stewed tomatoes. ❖ The tangy curry chicken has a hint of coconut milk and lime; its gravy is wonderful with rice. The curry goat, also a Jamaican staple, is almost a stew; the chunks of meat are tender and slightly garlicky. ❖ I'm a fried plantain fanatic, and these are fantastic, served piping hot, slightly mushy and sweet. They aren't greasy, as is often the case. Graham, a vegetarian, explains that his kitchen is health-conscious: He uses as little oil as possible and no MSG. ❖ Back to that dessert. We detest American fruit cake, with its hard little red and green things and all hideous manner of shriveled-up fruit. But Graham's mother urged us to give her version ($3.50) a try, so we did, gingerly. Surprise! It was dark, rich, and moist. ❖ The cake has a wonderful flavor of Jamaican rum, which Cynthia uses liberally — before, during, and after baking. The sweet white topping with a layer of almond paste was, well, icing on the cake.

BELLA ENGLISH, *Globe Staff*

# Broadway Diner

*117 Broadway, Arlington*
*781-316-1692.*
*Visa and MasterCard only.*
*Entry wheelchair accessible, bathrooms are not.*

**PRICES** *$2.25-$9.95.*

**HOURS** *Mon-Sat 6:30 a.m.-3 p.m., Sun 7 a.m.- 2 p.m. (only breakfast on Sunday)*

**ALCOHOL** *None.*

WEEK **49**

### HEY, TRY THESE

Pancakes (especially chocolate chip or apple-cinnamon), vegetarian omelet, Challah French toast with mixed fruit, egg salad.

**TASTING NOTES**

BOSTON • CAMBRIDGE

**WHEN NEW OWNERS TOOK OVER** the Arlington Restaurant & Diner, a longtime greasy spoon, a waitress named Carolina Guerrero decided to strike out on her own. With financial backing from her mom, she opened a rival restaurant about a half-mile away — and then hired a half-dozen waitresses from her former employer. ❖ With that, the Broadway Diner was open for business. And within six months this breakfast-and-lunch spot felt like a neighborhood veteran, thanks to the tight-knit staff. ❖ This is the kind of super family-friendly place where the sociable waitresses don't seem to mind when your 16-month-old nephew rolls grapes off the table and flings pancake onto the floor. ❖ For the most part, tradition reigns. Breakfast centers around eggs, home fries, pancakes, and waffles; lunch doesn't get much ritzier than tuna melts, grilled cheese sandwiches, and roast turkey clubs. ❖ But breakfast is the reason to come here. The tender buttermilk pancakes ($4.50, or short stack $3) are browned on the edges, and for an extra buck or two you can have chocolate chips, strawberries, blueberries, coconut, or walnuts pressed into the batter. The chocolate chip ones were so good that the 3-year-old even dreamt about them later, and I was crazy about my apple-cinnamon 'cakes ($6.95) oozing with sweet apple-pie filling. ❖ We were wowed by the variety of excellent sautéed veggies — red onions, spinach, tomato, mushroom, bell peppers, broccoli — in the fat, fluffy vegetarian omelet ($7.95). And our forks tangled as we jockeyed for bites of banana-nut French toast ($6.95) piled with sliced bananas and walnuts and Challah French toast ($7.50) heaped with beautiful fresh kiwi, mango, and pineapple. ❖ Lunch, though, was a series of disappointments. The bright spot was a deliciously chunky egg-salad sandwich ($3.75). But a BLT ($4.25) was made with a mealy tomato. Minestrone soup ($2.50/$3.50) was overly salty. A grilled chicken sandwich ($6.50) tasted totally unseasoned. Stuffed peppers, a daily special, were watery. A Reuben ($6.95) had a meager layer of corned beef and Swiss cheese that looked as if it had been peeled off a plastic wrapper. ❖ Then there was the feta cheese incident. Our feta-sprinkled Greek salad ($5.55) arrived with the unmistakably pungent odor of turned cheese. A nibble confirmed it. When we told our waitress, she took the salad away to consult with the cook, then returned with surprising news. ❖ "He says it's fine," she said apologetically. "I feel bad, but the owner's not here so I can't take it off the bill." ❖ The lesson: stick with breakfast. It's where the Broadway Diner excels.

SACHA PFEIFFER, *Globe Staff*

# Zaftigs

WEEK **50**

*335 Harvard St., Brookline (Coolidge Corner)*
*617-975-0075*
*www.zaftigs.com*
*All major credit cards accepted. Fully accessible.*
**PRICES** *$1.95 - $13.95.*
**HOURS** *Daily 8 a.m.-10 p.m.*
*Closed Thanksgiving and Christmas.*
**ALCOHOL** *Beer and wine.*

### HEY, TRY THESE

Potato pancakes, chicken soup, Cobb salad, roast chicken, Reuben sandwich.

**TASTING NOTES**

BOSTON • CAMBRIDGE

**ZAFTIGS DELICATESSEN OPENED** in 1997 in Brookline's Coolidge Corner, and there isn't anyone who knows the town well who doesn't compare the restaurant to the legendary Jack & Marion's, which was down the block for more than 20 years. Two of the three senior women in my group one night said, "This is just like Jack & Marion's," while another said, "This is nothing like Jack & Marion's." ❖ In fact, Zaftigs isn't like Jack & Marion's, the big Jewish delicatessen founded by Jack Solomon that closed in 1971. Zaftigs isn't as traditional, and though some dishes are wonderfully Old World, others have the unmistakable taste of chemicals. ❖ A perfectly good meatloaf ($13.95), for instance, which came with mushroom gravy and a terrific slaw, was drowned in a dark sauce that tasted as it if had been enhanced with Gravy Master. Owner Bob Shuman says on the phone a few days later (a little sheepishly), the sauce was probably made with something called "gravy base." Chicken soup ($3.50 a cup, $4.50 a pint, also available by the quart), which was practically spilling out of the bowl with a large, tender matzo ball, chunks of sweet carrot, and strips of moist chicken, had a broth that was a little too golden. The soup, made from kosher chickens, says Shuman, "sometimes" contains chicken base. ❖ Many items on the menu are very appealing. Meatless beet borscht ($3.50-$4.50) was deep scarlet, slightly sweet and sour, and a fine version of the classic. Potato pancakes ($8.50 for three) had crunchy exteriors and soft interiors. Soft and cheesy blintzes ($6.95) were like pillows, albeit with a fruit compote accompaniment that was too sweet. Zaftigs's meat knishes ($4.95 for two) were very different from the ones generally made in this region. These pastry-wrapped dumplings were filled with bits of pastrami and oddments of meat in the kitchen, flavorful but a little dry. Little scoops of chopped liver ($7.50) came with very thin bagel chips. The same crisp chips, made from all kinds of Zeppy's bagels, are set down with a cream-cheese spread when diners arrive. ❖ An ample Cobb salad ($12.95), brimming with crumbled bacon, morsels of turkey, chopped eggs, and avocado, was a treat. So was a roasted half chicken ($13.95) with steamed vegetables. And the Reuben sandwich ($12.50) was perfect: corned beef and Swiss cheese with sauerkraut and Russian dressing inside toasted pumpernickel. With one of the best half-sour pickles I've eaten in ages ($1.95 for a side order), the superb sandwich was indeed as good as the old Jack & Marion's.

SHERYL JULIAN, *Globe Staff*

# Deli After Dark

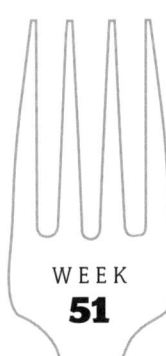

WEEK **51**

*545 High St., Dedham*
*781-326-9863*
*www.deliafterdark.com*
*All major credit cards accepted.*
*Wheelchair accessible.*
**PRICES** *$4.95-$11.95.*
**HOURS** *Wed-Fri 6 p.m.-midnight, Sat 4 p.m.-midnight (kitchen closes at 10 every night).*
**ALCOHOL** *Beer, wine, and cordials.*

### HEY, TRY THESE

Kimmie's shrimp skewers, honeymustard chicken wings, Kat's butternut-squash ravioli, Asian-noodle chicken salad, flatbread pizza.

**TASTING NOTES**

BOSTON • CAMBRIDGE

**THE CENTRE DELI IN DEDHAM** is a homegrown Cinderella story. By day, it's your ordinary delicatessen, serving up sandwiches and salads to those on the run. By night — at least Wednesday through Saturday — it is transformed into Deli After Dark. Those glass cases with sodas and juices are covered with a black curtain; a bartender appears; new menus materialize; three flat-screen TVs come alive with sports; and couples and families linger at tables over appetizers, entrees, and desserts. ❖ The change is seamless. But the spot, which has been in the Caruso family since 1959, has undergone many transformations over the years, according to Ernie Caruso, 52, whose parents bought it nearly 50 years ago. There are several high-top tables and some longer ones over which ceiling fans rotate lazily. ❖ Start with Kimmie's shrimp skewers ($7.95), eight fresh, plump shrimp grilled with a tad of ranch/Dijon sauce that has a sweet-and-sour tang to it. The chicken wings ($6.95) come three ways: We ordered honey mustard. They came nicely glazed and piping hot, with a chunky blue cheese dressing on the side. For dinner, we tried PaPa's Pesto Ravioli ($9.95), which consisted of several large orbs nicely stuffed with ricotta and drizzled with a pesto sauce. Though the pasta was cooked to just the right tenderness, the ricotta cheese was bland, and we could have used more sauce with added oomph — but maybe PaPa was more health conscious than we are. A better choice is Kat's butternut-squash ravioli ($10.95), with a light Alfredo sauce that carried a hint of nutmeg and lots of toasted walnuts. ❖ The flatbread pizzas are popular here, for good reason. The crust is almost cracker-thin, and the one we got — Carney's Meat Mop ($7.95) — was really loaded with pepperoni, sausage, and hamburger, with onions and mushrooms to assuage the guilt. The Buffalo Willie Pizza ($7.95) is fun and tasty, with buffalo chicken, red onion, and cheddar and blue cheeses. ❖ The service here is like the restaurant itself: friendly and casual. When a slice of our pizza slid off the tray in the kitchen, our waiter brought us the pizza minus the piece, and soon brought out another half pizza for us. ❖ Deli After Dark also offers sandwiches and salads. There are only two desserts on the menu: chocolate tornado cake and cheesecake (both $4.95). But both times we dined there, they were out. We'll be back for dessert, and for NaNa's Sunday Classic ($9.95), the Caruso matriarch's meatballs and sauce. We're anxious to see how it stacks up against PaPa's Pesto Ravioli.

BELLA ENGLISH, *Globe Staff*

# Shangri-La

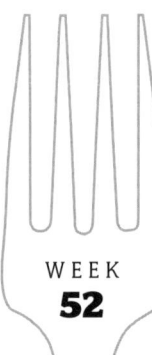

WEEK **52**

*149 Belmont St., Belmont*
*617-489-1488*
*MasterCard and Visa accepted.*
*One step at the door.*

**PRICES** *Appetizers and soups: $1.50-$9. Rice, noodles, and entrees: $2-$15.95 (most menu items are less than $11).*

**HOURS** *lunch Tue-Sun 11:30 a.m.-3 p.m. (Saturday and Sunday, dim sum)*
*dinner Tue-Thu 5-9:30 p.m., Fri-Sat 5-10 p.m., Sun 4-9:30 p.m.*

**ALCOHOL** *Wine and beer.*

### HEY, TRY THESE

Pan-fried white turnip cake, bean-curd skin rolls, spicy eggplant, three delight with flat noodles, jumbo meatballs with Chinese vegetables, crispy shrimp with spice salt.

**TASTING NOTES**

---

BOSTON • CAMBRIDGE

**HERE'S HOW MY FRIEND ORDERS** food at his favorite local spot, Shangri-La: He looks around for a table where at least two generations of Chinese families are eating (this is easy here) and asks the waitress to bring him several of the dishes they ordered. ❖ That's how we found our way to bean-curd skin rolls ($6.75), a cold appetizer. Not especially enticing, you're thinking. But they're terrific. Paper-thin skins, which have the quality and texture of a thin omelet, are wrapped around crisp bean sprouts and served with a spicy peanut sauce. Another dish we notice is white turnip cakes ($3.50), pureed roots shaped with rice flour into plump rounds and pan-fried. Think of them as Taiwanese risotto cakes. ❖ Jumbo meatballs arrive in a mound, surrounded by a circle of bright, steamed baby bok choy ($8.75). The only sauce on the plate is cooking juices from the steamed meat. "Three delight" with flat noodles ($6.25) is a kind of chow foon: Shrimp, squid, and chicken are tossed with the noodles and a soy-based sauce. It goes well with spicy eggplant ($8.25), thick meaty strips of vegetable in a fiery sauce. ❖ The six-year-old Shangri-La is owned by the Huang family. Sze Feng and Ann run the restaurant with their three sons. Wei, works at the restaurant after his day job in finance. John, who goes to the University of Massachusetts at Amherst, is learning the business at his father's side. And Jeffrey, a student at Suffolk, works at the restaurant on weekends. ❖ On the phone, John Huang says, "We try to make everything to order. We don't have heat lamps in our kitchen. That's why some items take a little longer." Indeed, when we ask for a steamed vegetable bun ($1.50 for one), we're told it will take 20 minutes. A very hot, airy round arrives, a filling of cabbage, shiitakes, and tofu tucked inside tender white dough. Crispy shrimp ($10.50), tails intact, are fanned along their curves; they're quite juicy, and terrific dipped into a little dish of salt spiked with hot pepper. ❖ Shangri-La is a little like visiting Chinatown. The lights are too bright, and the 40-seat place always boasts a full house, especially on weekends for dim sum, and even early on weeknights. But the friendly staff moves tables and chairs around to accommodate large families or couples, and children are always running around. ❖ In any case, you're usually quite close to the people beside you. Which is good if you want to peer over at their orders to see what to get.

SHERYL JULIAN, *Globe Staff*

## ARLINGTON
Broadway Diner (pancakes) ........................................................100
Rio Brazilian Barbeque (Brazilian) .............................................76

## BELMONT
Kitchen on Common (homestyle) ............................................78
Pho and Thai (Thai) ........................................................................34
Shangri-La (Chinese) ..................................................................106

## BOSTON
303 Cafe (eclectic) .........................................................................38
Bangkok Cafe, Roslindale (Thai) ................................................64
*Brown Sugar Cafe, Fenway (Thai) ............................................88
The Carving Station (sandwiches) ............................................36
Chipotle Mexican Grill, Brighton (Mexican) ............................42
Dino's, North End (Italian) ..........................................................22
El Oriental De Cuba, Jamaica Plain (Cuban) ...........................58
*El Pelon Taqueria, Fenway (Mexican) .....................................82
Esperia Grill & Rotisserie, Brighton (Greek) ............................26
*Flour Bakery + Cafe, South End (bakery) ..............................50
Gitlo's Dim Sum Bakery, Allston (Chinese) .............................40
Lorenz Island Kuisine, Dorchester (Jamaican) ......................98
*Original Kelly's Landing (beach food) ...................................28
Saray Restaurant (Turkish) .........................................................72
Sophia's Cafe (homestyle) ..........................................................32
Suvarnabhumi Kiri, Allston (Cambodian) ................................96
Viva Mi Arepa, West Roxbury (Venezuelan) ...........................16
*Wonder Spice Cafe, Jamaica Plain (Asian) ............................70
Z Square in the Park (lunch) ......................................................36

## BROOKLINE
*Dok Bua Thai Kitchen (Thai) .....................................................54
Orinoco (Venezuelan) ....................................................................6
Tashi Delek (Tibetan) ....................................................................66
*Zaftigs (deli) ...............................................................................102

BOSTON · CAMBRIDGE

## CAMBRIDGE

Annapurna (Himalayan) .................................................. 4
*Cambridge, 1 (pizza) ..................................................... 62
*Emma's (pizza) ............................................................. 48
Four Burgers (burgers) ................................................... 10
Good Food Cafe (homestyle) ......................................... 84

## MEDFORD

Tom Yum Koong Thai Cuisine (Thai) ............................. 20

## NEWTON

Pie Bakery & Cafe (slices) .............................................. 60

## SOMERVILLE

Alfresco (brunch/Mediterranean) ................................. 68
Ball Square Cafe & Breakfast (breakfast) ..................... 56
City Slicker Cafe (pizza) ................................................. 92
Machu Picchu Charcoal Chicken & Grill (Peruvian) .... 24
Pescatore Seafood (fish) ............................................... 86
Snappy Sushi (Japanese) ............................................... 46

## FARTHER OUT

Cafe Bistro, Natick (eclectic) ......................................... 74
Deli After Dark, Dedham (casual) ............................... 104
*Deluxe Town Diner, Watertown (diner) ...................... 94
Falafel King, Quincy (Middle Eastern) ............................ 8
The Fat Cat, Quincy (gastropub) ................................... 44
The Four's, Quincy (bar food) ....................................... 30
Jury Room, Quincy (eclectic) ......................................... 12
La Siesta Restaurante, Winthrop (Mexican) ................ 14
Peppercornz On Main, South Weymouth (Italian) ...... 52
Shiraz Cuisine, Watertown (Persian) ............................ 18
Taso's Euro-Cafe, Norwood (Greek) ............................. 90
Viet Grill, Canton (Vietnamese) .................................... 80

\* From the Cheap Eats Hall of Fame Archives

# 3 EASY STEPS TO BOSTON'S BEST MEALS

# 1 POINT
Go to boston.com/restaurants.

# 2 PLAN
Search by cuisine, price or location; read reviews; make reservations or get directions.

# 3 PIG OUT
Enjoy your meal. And please come again!

## boston.com
### For locals. By locals.

**✱ BURP (optional)**
After you've dined, add your own review to our restaurant listings.